Advance Praise for *Drama Free*

"Without a fresh perspective and the belief that we can break the cycle, we can get stuck in family patterns rather than living as our whole selves. With compassion and clarity, Nedra Tawwab offers a much-needed guide to understanding our upbringing—and becoming an agent for change in our own lives."

—Lori Gottlieb, *New York Times* bestselling author of *Maybe You Should Talk to Someone* and cohost of the *Dear Therapists* podcast

"In *Drama Free*, therapist Nedra Tawwab gives us the tools to understand family relationships and manage them in a healthier way—while staying true to who we are and what we need. This book offers a powerful path forward."

—Charlamagne Tha God, *New York Times* bestselling author and cohost of *The Breakfast Club*

"Many people go to therapy to work through the issues in their heads, overlooking that their biggest challenges often lie in their family relationships. In this book, therapist Nedra Tawwab offers practical wisdom to help you handle problems with parents, siblings, children, and yes, even in-laws. In a time when mental health is finally getting the attention it deserves, this is a vital guide to building healthier families."

—Adam Grant, #1 *New York Times* bestselling author of *Think Again* and host of the TED podcast *Re:Thinking*

"*Drama Free* is an engaging and relatable guide to understanding what's really going on within our families, offering practical steps for creating healthy changes as needed."   —Myleik Teele, founder of CURLBOX

"The family dynamics we grew up with can feel like an immutable fact of life—a set of patterns and rules we carry with us, for better or worse. In this empowering book, Nedra Tawwab upends this assumption, unpacking these complex relationships and offering tools for positive change."

—Judson Brewer, MD, PhD, *New York Times* bestselling author of *Unwinding Anxiety*

DRAMA
FREE

DRAMA
FREE

A Guide to Managing
Unhealthy Family Relationships

NEDRA GLOVER TAWWAB

A TarcherPerigee Book

tarcherperigee

an imprint of Penguin Random House LLC
penguinrandomhouse.com

Most TarcherPerigee books are available at special quantity discounts for bulk purchase for sales
promotions, premiums, fund-raising, and educational needs. Special books or book excerpts also can
be created to fit specific needs. For details, write: SpecialMarkets@penguinrandomhouse.com.

Hardcover ISBN 9780593539279
Ebook ISBN 9780593539286

Printed in the United States of America
1st Printing

For us, people who need to learn to manage or leave unhealthy family relationships—we are the answer, not the people we can't control

Contents

Contents

DRAMA
FREE

Introduction

Among the most significant contributors to your mental health, relationships can cause you pain, or they can heal you. Positively or negatively, relationships have an impact on your mental and emotional well-being. Psychologists have long supported the finding that healthy relationships can prolong your life, while unhealthy ones can influence health issues like cancer, heart disease, depression, anxiety, and addiction. So, we must take the health of our relationships seriously and strengthen connections where possible. While this applies to all types of relationships, no type of relationship is as formative as those we have with our family of origin.

My first book, *Set Boundaries, Find Peace: A Guide to Reclaiming Yourself,* helped people understand the importance of boundaries in relationships. Healthy boundaries give you peace even when the other person hasn't changed. They can help you deal with challenges and chaos in relationships. While this book doesn't focus on boundaries, they are frequently highlighted as a way to thrive in family relationships.

When people enter therapy, family relationships are most often what they want to discuss. From a therapist's perspective, many of the issues in marriages, friendships, and other relationships were birthed in our families. People may lament, "Not everything is about my family," but so often it is.

One question that often comes up in therapy is "Who was the first person to make you feel that way?" The answer typically goes back to the first experience occurring in the family. How people engage in the family is usually how they engage in the world.

Family relationships are the most common type of unhealthy relationship. If you're wondering why, I will venture to say that they are where we spend our formative years and a considerable amount of time (if not physically, then mentally). The people in our childhood home are our primary teachers for many years. But what happens when we want to show up in the world with views, traditions, or a lifestyle that diverges from those of our family? It can create tension and resentment.

The truth is that during your childhood, you likely weren't allowed to be yourself, so as an adult, you're becoming more your true self. And it's healthy for you to figure out who you are, separate from who you were molded or told to be. If this does cause friction, don't worry. In this book, I'll cover how to be yourself around your family.

Some people will say, "My childhood has no impact on who I am today." Not true. You can't simply extract all the good behaviors you learned and pretend away the ones you'd rather not possess. Behaviors stick to you until you consciously change them. Tendencies within families have a way of tricking us into accepting certain family norms. For instance, I've found that people from single-parent homes often struggle to understand the parent-child dynamics when two parents are involved. When they have a partner to support them in parenting, it can be hard for them to understand and embrace the involvement of another adult.

Of course, there's no such thing as a "perfect" childhood. Even when it appears fine from the outside, we have no clue what's going on behind closed doors. For some of us, the most complicated relationships we have are with our family. People tell me that they want to change or improve their family relationships—especially with parents, siblings, and extended family members such as grandparents, aunts, uncles, and cousins—more than any other relationships. Another huge sore point is our relationship with in-laws and blended family members, such as learning to parent children who have become adults. Plus, family relationships set the tone for how we operate in outside relationships, including friendships and romantic relationships.

When I offer relationship solutions, people often ask if my advice applies to family—it does. I know it can be hard to apply general knowledge to family relationships. When it's family, we might make an unhealthy exception because—it's family. But we shouldn't make that mistake. Don't allow anyone to mistreat you, no matter who they are.

This book is not for blaming other people for your life. Instead, it's a tool to help you develop the skills needed to reclaim your voice in a dysfunctional family. It can be scary to face what you witnessed or endured in your family. I, too, at times have avoided or downplayed family issues as a way to keep family norms intact. Often, people avoid being honest about their family experiences because they fear challenging conversations or possibly feeling the need to leave their family behind. Releasing family relationships is only one option of many, and having tough but intentional conversations can create positive change.

I will teach you how to manage dysfunctional family relationships better, and how to sever ties when those relationships become unmanageable. You don't have to tolerate toxic behavior from others, but you might not have to cut people off. This depends on your tolerance and grace, and the intensity of the offending behavior. Dysfunction is not just abuse or neglect; it's also gossiping, unhealthy in-law relationships, feeling like the black sheep, or dealing with a substance-abusing family member.

Indeed, I will offer practical tips for common issues and succinctly break down complex topics, helping you to answer two essential questions:

- How can I successfully have relationships with members of my family when there's an underlying issue?
- How can I disconnect from family members when I no longer wish to maintain the relationship?

Keep a notebook handy or your notes app open, because as you read, it will be helpful to reflect, process, and apply the experiences in this book to your life. Writing is cathartic and can help you sort through thoughts in a deeper way.

In **Part One: Unlearning Dysfunction**, I'll explain what dysfunction looks like and define typical unhealthy dynamics, including trauma, boundary violations, codependency, enmeshment, and addiction. We'll explore why people tend to repeat chaos and continue unhealthy patterns, as well as the impact of generational trauma.

In **Part Two: Healing**, I'll delve into the two choices you have when you want to break the cycle: learn how to manage relationships with people who won't change, or end relationships because people won't change. This section offers guidance for thriving vs. surviving and for building a support system outside your family.

Part Three: Growing will help you troubleshoot the different types of family relationships: parents, siblings, extended family, adult children, in-laws, and blended families.

While reading this book, if you begin to uncover parts of the story that cause you to feel overwhelmed, seek therapy to address those issues. Significant reactions are a sign that something deeper is being experienced, and therapy can help explore the deeper reactions, such as loss of sleep,

re-experiencing, racing thoughts, or intense sadness. Therapy is a supportive process that can help you work through the topics in this book, particularly when processing on your own becomes unmanageable. This book
is a therapeutic, educational tool and in no way takes the place of having
a relationship with a therapist if you need one. If something doesn't feel
right for you or you don't have access to therapy and you're having an emotional reaction, pause when needed and return to the material when you
feel more equipped to process it.

Each chapter opens with a quote and vignette loosely based on an interaction with a client or member of my Instagram community. From there,
the chapters move into clinical concepts and scripts, and end with an exercise of reflective questions to help you apply the material to your real-life
experiences. Throughout this book, the term "parent" is used to refer to a
biological parent, primary caregiver, adoptive parent, or any adult who was
primarily responsible for your care. To protect the identity of current and
former clients, names and details have been changed. Many of the stories
are composites and rearranged details from my personal and professional
lives.

Culture impacts our views of family, and in some cultures, speaking up
against unhealthy family practices or wanting something different could
seem to be going against your cultural values. Adults can create their own
identities, even in family relationships. You are allowed to change aspects
of the existing culture in your family—such as visiting without advance
notice, taking care of elderly parents while raising your own children, or
giving unqualified family members roles in your business. You have the
power to create your own story while allowing your family to maintain
their culture. You aren't being offensive; you are simply trying to create a
life that fits your desires.

The relationships that impact us the most are those with family. The
wounds are deep, and the relationships are filled with expectations.

Whether you consider your family truly dysfunctional or just want to re-solve some drama, I hope reading this book will show you that you aren't alone and that you have the power to decide what you want in your rela-tionships with others. You can choose how to live your life. Believe that you have everything within yourself to make hard and healthy decisions. I know you can do this because I've witnessed many others, including my-self, create healthy relationships.

PART ONE

UNLEARNING DYSFUNCTION

CHAPTER 1

What Dysfunction Looks Like

Carmen grew up in a two-parent home. It was customary for her father, Bruce, to work all day, come home, get drunk, and go into a rage. Carmen's mom, April, spent much of her time in her room disengaged from Carmen and her two siblings. April "drank too much," but she wasn't as bad as Bruce.

When April and Bruce would argue, Carmen and her siblings would tune them out by blasting the TV. Carmen spent a lot of time with her friends to avoid being at home. With her friends' families, she found that it wasn't the norm for parents to be drunk, argue all the time, or be emotionally neglectful.

As Carmen grew older, she learned to rely on her extended family for support. When she needed a ride to hang out with friends, she'd call her grandmother. She couldn't risk her parents picking her up while drunk. When she needed clothes for school, she called her aunt, who gladly took her shopping. What Carmen didn't have was someone to talk to about her homelife. Her friends didn't have these issues with their parents, and her extended family danced around her parents' issues by trying to pick up the slack.

Carmen was lonely and embarrassed. For many years, she thought she was the problem because no one else seemed concerned about her parents' actions. Her siblings accommodated their parents' behavior, and the rest of the family said things like, "That's just who your parents are. You have to love them anyway." She loved her parents, but she was tormented by how they behaved. Their issues even continued into her adulthood.

Most of the time, Carmen just sucked it up, and when she did put her foot down, her family guilt-tripped her, accusing her of acting funny and being mean. She wanted someone to see the issues, validate her experiences, and let her know that it was OK to want something different from her family.

What Does It Mean to Have a Dysfunctional Family?

For Carmen, it meant having parents who were addicts, emotionally neglectful, and at times verbally abusive. A dysfunctional family is one where abuse, chaos, and neglect are accepted norms. In dysfunctional families, unhealthy behaviors are overlooked, swept under the rug, or catered to. As in Carmen's case, it's hard to ascertain dysfunction until you're exposed to other, healthier situations. And even when exposed to better relationships, it can still be hard to break away from dysfunctional patterns.

If you grew up in a dysfunctional family, you probably thought this was normal:

- Forgiving and forgetting (with no change in behavior)
- Moving on as if nothing happened
- Covering up problems for others
- Denying that a problem exists
- Keeping secrets that need to be shared
- Pretending to be fine

- Not expressing your emotions
- Being around harmful people
- Using aggression to get what you want

When People Tell You There's a Problem, Believe Them

Far too often, people become defensive and resistant to change instead of acknowledging the problem and working toward a resolution. In Carmen's case, whenever she tried to talk to her parents about some of their unhealthy behaviors, they became defensive or blamed her for wanting something different. No one within the family was willing to hear her concerns, likely because they weren't ready to work on the issues.

Carmen wasn't alone, yet no one was willing to stand with her. Her experience was the same as everyone else's, but she was the one who was brave enough to point out that there was a problem. She wanted to learn how to confront the issues that everyone seemed to easily accommodate or ignore.

Adverse Childhood Experiences (ACE) Survey

The Adverse Childhood Experiences (ACE) Survey is commonly used to measure the severity of childhood trauma. The survey takes into consideration areas such as these:

Witnessing violence

Sexual abuse

Exposure to substance abuse in the home

Physical abuse

Verbal abuse

Emotional abandonment

Parent who was mentally ill

Imprisonment of a parent

Childhood trauma impacts our ability to process and express emotions, and it increases the likelihood of maladaptive emotional-regulation strategies (e.g., suppression of emotions). In particular, children exposed to violence have challenges in distinguishing threat and safety cues.

It's widely known that things like abuse and neglect are dysfunctional aspects within a family dynamic. But family relationships are impacted by other factors as well. Trauma is assessed on a scale from 0 to 10, but childhood trauma can be impactful with a score as low as 2. ACE doesn't even consider financial instability, moving multiple times, or generational trauma, which we know impact mental health. I believe that your ACE score (mine is a 7) or childhood experience of trauma doesn't determine your future. We are powerful and can make choices that are hard in the moment but beneficial in the long term.

What we experience in childhood carries over to adulthood because once the trauma is activated, the cycle is often perpetuated. Children who experience homelessness tend to have higher ACE scores and a higher likelihood of homelessness issues in adulthood.

Other Factors That Contribute to Childhood Dysfunction

- Self-absorbed parents
- Emotionally immature parents
- Domineering parents
- Enmeshed family relationships
- Competitive relationships within the family
- Children parenting their parents

(In Chapters 2 and 3, we will dig deeper into these concepts.)

A compelling documentary, *The Boys of Baraka* is about a program with Black boys in Baltimore, Maryland. Twenty at-risk young men enrolled in a boarding school in Kenya to experience their cultural roots, community, academics, and structure. While away, many of the boys showed improvements academically, emotionally, and socially. The program then lost funding, and the boys returned home. Once they returned to their home environments, which hadn't changed, many of them suffered the consequences of growing up in these at-risk environments, including drug abuse, jail, and repeating unhealthy cycles. The atmosphere in which they lived limited their ability to thrive, and with little hope, they returned to familiar patterns.

Nevertheless, with the right tools, we can heal from childhood and family traumas.

Environment

Where you grow up, who you grow up with, and the things you experience in your home have lifelong implications for who you become. Trauma has long-term effects on your body, mind, relationships, financial health, and emotional and mental health. The first eighteen years of life profoundly impact your entire life. In the book *What Happened to You?: Conversations on Trauma, Resilience, and Healing,* by Oprah Winfrey and Bruce D. Perry, M.D., Ph.D., Oprah shares her story of childhood trauma and how those experiences shaped her. Her mother beat her for even the slightest offense, and this abuse turned her into a people-pleaser. It took years for her to realize that her behavior as an adult was rooted in her experiences as a child.

Things You May Inherit from Your Family
- Money management skills
- Communication skills
- The way you attach to others

- Values
- Patterns of substance use
- How you treat your children
- How you handle your mental health

There's so much from your childhood that gives therapists a picture of how you developed the problem you're working through in adulthood. One thing I ask is, "When is the first time you felt that way?" or "Who was the first person to make you feel that way?" Typically, the narrative floats back to childhood. We carry the weight of the years when we were most powerless, as if we have to continue that way, but adulthood gives us the opportunity to change our narrative.

Adulthood gives us the opportunity to change our narrative.

Resilience

Resilience is the ability to embrace what happened. We can overcome our environment when the right protective factors are in place. Protective factors include

- Strong connections with safe adults
- Positive parenting influences
- Strong values or a sense of purpose
- The ability to self-regulate, have a positive outlook, and be resourceful
- Healthy social connections
- Support from peers and mentors
- Continual structured programs that increase exposure to healthy relationships

It's often said that we are a product of our environment, but we can also be a product of exposure to healthy relationships outside the home. Carmen's understanding of her home environment was shaped by what she saw as healthy alternatives outside her home.

Growing up in Detroit, Michigan, and attending public schools, I recall being exposed to programs intended to help urban kids overcome issues they may have faced at home. I stopped littering in elementary school because a group taught us about how littering is harmful to our environment, and they helped us clean the neighborhood around my school. Although the cleaning efforts were short-lived, the piece about not littering stuck with me.

Strangers have assumed that I was raised in a two-parent home and that my childhood was free of trauma, but neither of those assumptions is true. I had exposure to different perspectives and healthy relationships, and I hoped that my life would be different when I became an adult.

Be Honest (at Least with Yourself) About Your Childhood

Honesty isn't betrayal; it's courage. Stop sugarcoating your experiences and allow the truth to free you. People often misrepresent their relationships and experiences because they're too afraid to admit what's true. But denial will keep you from breaking free from your past.

Hard Things to Accept About a Family Member
- They are selfish and will do whatever it takes to get what they want
- They aren't a good listener
- They make changes, but only temporarily
- They are mean, often without cause

- They take more than they give
- They aren't perfect

Reasons We Don't Talk About Family Problems

Thinking That Family Issues Are a Reflection of Who We Are

You aren't what happened to you. In childhood, you faced many things that were outside your control. Managing your environment wasn't on you. Therefore, you can't blame yourself for what happened in that environment. Your experiences shaped you—but as an adult, you have the

You aren't what happened to you.

power to choose whether you want to be a product of those experiences or move past them to create something different.

Feeling Embarrassment and Shame

One thing that helps with feeling embarrassed about your family story is hearing about people with similar experiences. The only way to connect with those who share your experiences, however, is honesty. You will have to be brave enough to tell the truth. Shame exists when you hide things from others, and releasing the secrets releases shame. Maintaining privacy is not secret-keeping; you can share as much or as little as you feel comfortable sharing. Privacy allows you to discern whom you prefer to disclose to. Sometimes you don't share as a protection to the people who harmed you. Therefore, you might be engaging in preventing embarrassment for others, not just for yourself.

Trying to Ignore the Issues

Ignoring major family issues postpones the healing of unhealthy patterns. You can't recover from things that "never happened." When you ignore them, the harmful behaviors continue because you and your family are unwilling to acknowledge the cycles that need to be recognized and broken.

Ignoring major family issues postpones the healing of unhealthy patterns.

Believing That No One Will Understand

Celebrities, teachers, friends, coworkers, and many others might have gone through similar issues with their families. Assuming you're alone isn't the best way to find people who can relate to you. Vulnerability builds community. You attract people who are like you by being authentic and open. Sometimes, you find "your people" after you are transparent about your story.

Fearing Judgment

Some people won't understand your story, and you won't always understand the stories of others. Practice feeling OK with the fact that some people won't "get" you. Accepting this will make your life much easier. It makes sense to be concerned about what others think. But caring too much can undermine your ability to create positive change.

Watching the Trauma Unfold

Married... with Children was one of my favorite TV sitcoms. In it, Al Bundy, the main character, is a disgruntled shoe salesman whose best years were in high school. He's married to Peg, and they have two kids, named Bud and Kelly. The kids watch as their parents criticize each other, and they are often left at home without food to eat. I recall one episode where the kids are hungry and searching the kitchen for food. They find an old piece of chocolate behind the refrigerator and rejoice. The show is a comedy, and I found many of the dynamics hilarious. But in hindsight, I realize the show highlights aspects of parental neglect, verbal abuse, and unhealthy parental relationships that I couldn't yet conceptualize.

When we don't understand what we see, we tend to stay in unhealthy situations. It can feel normal and inevitable that the people around us seem to suffer the same fate. To better understand your experience, it's vital to develop a different viewpoint.

What Happens When It Takes Years to Wake Up

As long as you are breathing, it isn't too late to change your perspective and behaviors. It's commonly believed that the older we become, the more challenging it might be to change. They say, "You can't teach an old dog new tricks." Not true! When you're willing to incorporate further information, you can change. Let's revise the saying to "You can't teach an *unwilling* dog new tricks." In reading this book, you've demonstrated that you're willing to seek out and incorporate new information.

Sometimes, the problems are blatantly obvious, but because of the indoctrination of family values and beliefs, it can take a while before you start to realize the nature of the dysfunction in your family. Like Carmen, however, you can begin to observe others and notice the differences in your home.

My own after-school routine included watching *The Oprah Winfrey Show*. As I've watched old episodes, I realize now that I wasn't ready for the topics, but I certainly needed to hear them. The Oprah show covered abuse, neglect, giveaways, celebrity interviews, and almost every other imaginable subject. Her show gave me the terminology to name things in my life and the lives of others. If you listen closely enough, many of the things you watch and read contain something about your experiences in life. Media is one way we learn to connect what we see with our own situations.

But it's never too late to start rewiring your brain. You're always learning new things, and choosing to incorporate new ideas is a choice you can make. Throughout this book, I will teach you how to change yourself in order to change your life and relationships. You are a huge part of all your relationships. Therefore, your perspective, behaviors, and expectations can often change how a relationship functions, even if the other person doesn't change.

You'll hear me repeat one concept in this book: *You cannot change people.* If I could have one superpower, it would be to change people. But none of us possess the power to change others. Nevertheless, it's the number one go-to solution when we have problems in relationships. After you read this book, I want you to walk away with the realization that changing *you* is enough.

Changing you *is enough.*

Starting from Scratch

There's a scene in the movie *The Little Mermaid* where Ariel uses a fork as a comb. She's never seen a comb before, so she has no frame of reference for it. When your reference point is dysfunctional, changing to a healthier pattern will often involve starting from scratch. I've seen parents become shocked by how hard it is to break dysfunctional cycles with their own children. In this case, parents have options:

- Get upset with their children for being unreasonable and needy.
- Get upset with their parents for not having been more patient with *them*.
- Learn strategies to parent better and manage stress.

All of these options are reasonable. You can be upset while building parenting skills and managing the stress that comes with parenting. It's OK to feel upset, sad, or even angry about the past while you move forward with your life. Notice that I didn't say "getting over" the past. Instead, I emphasized moving forward.

There may be moments when revisiting the past upsets you, but don't stay there. Remember that you live in the present moment, and you can only *revisit* the past. You can't relive it or undo it. So spend most of your energy on making changes that will impact you in healthy ways today and in the future. Visit the past, but don't stay there.

Visit the past, but don't stay there.

We Do What We Know More Often Than We Learn Something New

"That's just how I am" is what people typically say when they aren't ready or willing to change. But we always have a choice to be different. The first key is awareness, and then being willing to take the first step to do something different. We don't have to repeat the same mistake twice.

Most of what you apply in adult relationships has been unconsciously learned by observing relationships in your family of origin or observing the relationships of your peers. Very few of us look at scientific data to figure out what works. In general, you repeat what you see. Modeling is how you learn to engage with the world around you. If you see your parents yelling at each other during a conflict, it makes sense that yelling is one of your go-to strategies.

Conversely, people may choose to avoid conflict altogether to avoid yelling, not realizing that they can respond differently in times of conflict. I've heard so many people say, "I hate conflict because I grew up watching my parents demean each other." Growing up with unhealthy examples leads us to believe that if we speak in an argument, we'll yell or be mean.

You Have a Choice

Before adulthood, your caregivers likely controlled your relationships with family members, friends, associates, and others. Once you become an adult (able to care for yourself independent of your parents, likely around ages eighteen to twenty-three), you can decide how you want to exist in your relationships with others and who you want to be with. Even when someone disagrees with a relationship you have with someone else, they can only give you their opinion. You have to manage the discomfort of the feedback, but other people can't manage your adult relationships for you.

It's always your choice. You can teach yourself things that you never learned as a child, you can choose to respond differently, and you can be yourself. Your superpower is your ability to decide how you wish to show up in the world.

How Childhood Issues Impact Adult Relationships

Family relationships can mimic the way you show up in other relationships. Family relationships can create the following issues:

Anxiety

> If it was customary to be anxious about the behavior of others in your family, you will be anxious about the behaviors of others in your relationships outside your family.

Imposter Syndrome

   If you were told or it was implied that you weren't enough, you will carry the message "I'm not worthy" with you wherever you go.

Struggles with Communicating Your Needs and Feelings

   If you were ridiculed, dismissed, or punished for sharing a need or simply showing a feeling, you will carry this programming with you in other relationships.

Self-Sabotage

   If you stay in a cycle of dysfunction, your feelings of unworthiness might cause you to unconsciously sabotage yourself from having good things or healthy relationships.

Trust Issues

   When the people who are supposed to love you unconditionally violate your trust, it can be difficult to believe other people could love you, be present, or care for you.

Commitment Issues

   Avoidance is a strategy that people use to keep themselves safe. If you've experienced unhealthy family relationships, it makes sense that you would fear building and nurturing connections with others.

Relationships Impact Your Mental Health

Mental health issues can be contagious and stressful. If you grow up in a home with depression, you will likely develop depression, not necessarily because it's genetic but because it's what you observed. Depressed parents engage with children differently, and they shape the child's physical and emotional outlook. This, in turn, leads children to develop some of the same characteristics exhibited by their parents.

It's the same way with anxiety. So many adults learn to be anxious by observing and being parented by anxious adults. You learn and practice what you see. Kids are very good at reading the emotional cues of adults. I've heard some adults say, "I could tell when my dad was drunk by the way he took his coat off." Kids intuitively read the room.

When you feel you have to intuit the emotions of others, however, it's stressful because you're constantly on guard. When you're an adult, the behavior of reading emotional cues can turn into a mistrust of others, a lack of vulnerability, or falling into the pattern of protecting others.

Mistrusting Others

Relationships can't be healthy when they lack trust. An integral part of a healthy relationship is believing that the other person will honor their commitment to you. The only way to learn to trust is to allow another person into your world and hope they'll live up to your expectations. It's scary to believe someone can be there for you when your primary caregivers betrayed your trust, but I assure you that it's possible to learn to trust. First, you have to learn to trust in your ability to choose healthy people.

Avoiding Vulnerability

It makes sense to guard your heart. But you can't protect yourself from disappointment. You can only try to anticipate it or avoid it. It makes sense to attempt to control the impact, but you won't be taken advantage of in healthy relationships. Therefore, work on picking healthy people so that you can let your guard down.

Protecting Others

Worrying about others might seem like a way to protect them, but it's stressful to you and offers them little help. You can't protect people from the damage they're doing to themselves. You can't watch them constantly and also live your life.

EXERCISE

Grab your journal or a piece of paper to complete the following prompts:

* What dysfunctional family patterns have you carried into adult relationships?
* Have you ever felt powerless in your ability to make changes within your family?
* Whom do you feel comfortable talking to about your upbringing, and why are you comfortable with that person?

CHAPTER 2

Boundary Violations, Codependency, and Enmeshment

The twins—that's how everyone still saw them even though they were thirty-two years old. People still thought of them as the same person. Even they had a hard time distinguishing their thoughts from each other's. The younger of the two, Briana, was getting married. Her fiancé, Thomas, complained that he felt like he was second in line to Chelsea, her twin sister. Whenever there was a decision to be made, Briana talked to Chelsea first. Thomas was concerned what their marriage would be like if Briana couldn't decide anything without first seeking guidance from her sister.

Although she was only five minutes older, Chelsea was the boss. Her number one priority was taking care of her little sister. Sometimes, Briana complained that Chelsea was overinvolved, but she always saw Chelsea's way eventually. Chelsea liked her soon-to-be brother-in-law, but she noticed that since Briana and Thomas had become engaged, Briana was more distant. Their twice-daily calls, multiple texts throughout the day, and Thursday-night sister-dates had changed to talking once a day or sometimes every other day, sporadic texting, and watching "our shows" together with Thomas on Thursdays instead of sister-dates. Chelsea could feel the changes happening. Meanwhile, Briana seemed happier than ever.

Chelsea came to therapy after she confronted her sister about the distance. It was the first time in their relationship that Briana's mind didn't change to do as "the boss" said. Chelsea accused Thomas of being controlling and trying to damage their relationship. In our work together, Chelsea explored boundaries, particularly how they are essential for people to establish healthy roles in their relationships.

Boundaries (My Favorite "B" Word)

Boundaries are expectations and needs that help us feel comfortable and safe in our relationships. Verbally and through your behaviors, you set boundaries with others. In dysfunctional families, the main way boundary issues appear is through codependency or enmeshment. In some instances, you might feel more comfortable creating behavioral boundaries, and at other times, you might verbalize your boundaries.

Briana created the following behavioral boundaries:

- Speaking to her sister less often
- Texting less frequently
- Cutting back on in-person gatherings
- Not being readily available for her sister's needs

For Briana, it seemed most manageable or less aggressive to create behavioral boundaries. If she had implemented verbal boundaries, it might have sounded like this: "Thomas and I are building a life together and determining what that looks like for us. You may notice that I'm less available." Or "I'm transitioning into a commitment, and I'll focus my attention on building a solid relationship with Thomas. For us, that might look like less chatting throughout the day." Or "I want more autonomy as an adult. Therefore, you'll see me engaging more in independent decision-making."

Chelsea could find any of these statements offensive simply because they threaten what she wants for her relationship with Briana. Alternatively, Chelsea could respect her sister's need for autonomy and desire to work on her relationship with Thomas, and she could develop new ways to support Briana.

What Happens When You Set Boundaries in a Dysfunctional Family?

Boundaries in unhealthy families are a threat to the ecosystem of dysfunction. Changes like new boundaries mean that dysfunctional systems are being challenged.

Disapproval

"It's not me; it's you," or in other words, "You're wrong for changing. Everything was going well until you intervened with your ideas about changing the status quo."

Change is a healthy part of relationships. No one stays the same, or at least it isn't beneficial to stay the same. From childhood to adulthood, we each become a different person. It isn't uncommon for us to become more comfortable exploring what we've long wanted to change when we gain the support to do so. These changes may manifest in friendships, in social spaces, at work, or in romantic relationships.

Briana seemed happy with building her relationships and enjoying different things. Although Chelsea wasn't used to this part of Briana, it doesn't mean that Thomas was the source of that change. Perhaps he provided a safe space for Briana to become something other than what her sister knew her to be.

Shame

"You're a terrible person."

Shame is an attack on your character, and it strikes at the core of your emotions. In dysfunctional families, shame is used as a control tactic. Typically, parents will place a rule, and when kids don't comply, the message is "you're terrible" or "you're bad."

Shame breeds guilt, and guilt moves people to compliance. Making someone seem like a terrible person for wanting something different is a form of control. It's healthy to want people to value your opinion, but it's unhealthy to disagree with someone and then attack their character.

Pushback (Resistance)

"I hear you, and I don't care."

Pushback involves completely disregarding someone's request, engaging in passive-aggressive or aggressive behavior, or challenging a request.

Pushback might look like this:

- Continuing to do what they were already doing
- Pressuring someone to change their mind
- Intimidating someone as a way to get them to change

Resentment

"I'm upset because you want something different."

Sadness, fear, hurt, and disappointment all rolled up into one become resentment. Underlying resentment is dangerous in relationships because flare-ups can happen when we least expect them. With Chelsea and Briana, if the issue isn't resolved, both of them will likely continue to struggle through the boundary challenges in their relationship.

Codependency

In healthy adult relationships, you don't have to be responsible for other people. The responsibility of managing someone else's life, mood, boundaries, and feelings is codependency. In unhealthy adult relationships, codependency can manifest as feeling entitled to access someone's life and how they choose to function in their life.

While needing people is healthy, enmeshing with them and losing who you are is codependent. Making it your job to rescue them from problems of their own doing (without being asked) is codependent. Losing touch with your needs and taking on someone else's is codependent. Mutual closeness is healthy, but entangling who you are and how you feel with someone else isn't.

Examples of Codependency
- Your brother loses his job, and without him asking, you start paying his rent because you know he'll need the help.
- Your mother abuses pain medication, and since you don't want her buying it off the street, you give her your pain medication.
- Your cousin calls to talk about her marriage, but instead of listening, you jump in with solutions and offer her a place to stay.

With codependency, you assume the other person needs your help. Sometimes, help may have been needed in the past, but the pattern of helping never stopped.

I remember when I used to be codependent:
- I made excuses for people.
- I cleaned up other people's messes.

- I tried to solve other people's problems.
- I neglected myself to take care of others.
- I worried about other people's problems as if they were my own.
- I tried to convince, persuade, or push people to change.
- I felt frustrated because people weren't changing.
- I helped people when I wasn't in a position to do so.
- I vented to people about other people's problems.
- I worked harder than the other person to find solutions to their problems.
- I minimized the impact others had on me because I didn't want to hurt them.

It's easy to fall into the pattern of taking care of people who are capable of taking care of themselves. Sometimes, the person you intend to help doesn't want to change. With each choice, you have the option to allow people to self-manage or to manage things for them. You can manage codependency by showing people how to care for themselves, allowing them to evolve into greater self-sufficiency, and managing the expectations of your support for them. When someone is misusing drugs, having financial problems, or negatively impacting their life, it might seem like taking over their problems is the only solution. But it's not.

Show People How to Care for Themselves

Someone on Instagram asked me the following question: "How do I get over the need to care for my siblings? I'm resentful, but I'm used to being in the role of caretaker. Now that we're adults, I continue to act as a parent to my siblings."

In childhood, perhaps you were in a home where adults didn't provide the necessary care, so you stepped up as a parentlike figure. But is this level of parenting still necessary? As adults, we must transition into the role of supportive sibling.

When people don't have the tools, show them how to do something instead of doing it for them. We often assume that doing things for people is the most helpful way to support them, but ultimately, showing them how to take care of themselves is the best way to help them in the long term. When we rob people of the ability to care for themselves, we sign ourselves up for a lifetime commitment to helping them. Hard truth: some people (including those we love) have no desire to care for themselves in healthy ways, or lack the will to do so.

Overhelping comes at a cost. Being there for others and not being present in our own life is stressful and impacts our mental health.

Allow People to Evolve

People are not who they used to be. Everyone gets older and becomes a little bit different. Family members morph into different people right in front of us. But sometimes, we don't shift how we see them from who they were to who they have become.

For a time, I was the youngest grandchild out of more than seven first cousins. Many of them saw/see me as the "baby." In many ways, it's delightful because my cousins have many fond memories of me as a baby and during my younger years. As I've grown up, I've heard, "I can't believe my baby is getting married," or "I can't believe my baby is moving to another state." Those sorts of comments are acceptable, but what about when people hear, "You're not ready to get married," or "You can't move away from your family"? Sometimes, the stories that other people have about us might stop us from pursuing the life we want.

From birth, you are growing and learning how to function in the world.

People can outgrow who you thought they were, but it's healthiest to grow with them. Stifling someone's growth by guilting them into staying the same leads them to make changes secretly or do so without loving support.

Manage Expectations

What are your boundaries? Indeed, you have an idea of potential ways to help and ways that helping might cost you. Before agreeing to assist others, deeply consider your boundaries, and remember that there are so many ways to support people. Make a list of what could be supportive outside of doing things for others. Beyond that, ask them the magical question "How can I support you?" Perhaps the person has something else in mind in terms of support. Make it a practice to ask before doing.

Say This to Yourself: "I can listen to people without assuming that my help is needed. It isn't my role to resolve issues that they can resolve on their own. If people want my help, I will allow them to ask. When asked to help, I will help in a way that doesn't take anything away from my care for myself."

Try these affirmations when you find yourself struggling with codependency.

- "I am learning to say no."
- "I am willing to allow others to take care of themselves."
- "I am becoming separate from others."
- "I am setting limits for myself."
- "I am releasing overinvolvement in other people's problems."
- "I am discovering that people can manage their own lives."
- "I am willing to step back and allow things to unfold."
- "I am deserving of self-care."
- "I am responsible for myself."

Enmeshment

Enmeshment is when there's no separation between yourself and others. Sharing the same perspective on all things, existing in the same way, and having very few boundaries are basic components of enmeshment.

In dysfunctional families, enmeshment allows everyone to stay the same, and when the status quo is challenged, the challenger becomes a scapegoat, rule breaker, and threat. A family is a cultural system. Sometimes, when individuals try to create new traditions, shift roles, or create boundaries, the system feels under attack.

A family is a cultural system.

Chelsea saw Briana's desire to have a separate identity as a threat to their twin-sister dynamic. As the oldest, Chelsea could control the relationship, but as Briana changed, Chelsea felt she was losing power. Chelsea needed to become comfortable with the changes in the relationship due to Briana's desire for more autonomy.

Examples of Enmeshment

- An adult child decides to become Muslim after being raised in a Christian household. All family members turn their back on the member who converts.
- A sibling attends college out of state and receives backlash from family for not attending school nearby.
- A daughter gets engaged, and her mother takes charge of the planning without considering her daughter's wishes or desires.

When searching for autonomy in adult family relationships, people often feel overwhelmed with guilt about going against the cultural system. Here are a few reminders for adults who feel conflicted:

*You can love your family and still be upset about things they did or
    didn't do.*

Both things can be true, and many relationships are complicated. When you open yourself up to the possibility that multiple feelings can coexist, it becomes easier for you to
acknowledge the positive and negative aspects of your relationships.

You can love your parents and be upset about how they raised you.

Often in relationships, you will feel upset or disappointed
by someone you love. To love someone is to be willing to
be hurt.

It's OK to have boundaries with your family.

Boundaries are a healthy part of all relationships. Maintain
limits and expectations with friends, romantic partners, work,
social media, family, and all other areas that impact your mental health.

Being assertive is not rude.

In an Instagram poll, I asked people, "What's something
that you did that someone labeled as rude?" People replied:

"I was called rude for saying that I didn't want to ride to the
store with someone."

"Someone asked me to borrow money, and I said no because
I didn't have it."

"My friend asked for my opinion, and I was honest."

Rudeness is intentionally sabotaging behaviors. For example, if you see someone trying to come in the door behind you,
and you deliberately close the door on them, that's rude.

Sometimes what we consider rude is actually just being honest, setting a limit, denying a request, thinking differently, or being assertive.

You are not a sellout or bougie for having views that differ from your family of origin's.
In an attempt to shame or control your behaviors, people may label you to try to make you feel bad enough to change.

When people disagree with you, it doesn't mean you're wrong.
You don't have to prove that you're right. I know it's hard to be misunderstood, but you have to become OK with the fact that some people won't understand you. Know that people (even those you love) might disagree with you.

To be healthy, you must manage what you can, but never other people and how they choose to live. Even when you love someone and believe you know what's best for them, you cannot control them.

Autonomy is a healthy part of relationships. A wonderful way to support others is to allow them to be as they are. Knowing you can choose how to help people frees you to develop your own ideas about what's possible in your relationships.

EXERCISE

Grab your journal or a piece of paper to complete the following prompts:

* How does codependency or enmeshment show up in your family relationships?

※ What happens in your family when someone goes against what's considered normal?

※ Is there anyone in your family who shares your view of the dysfunction?

CHAPTER 3

Addiction, Neglect, and Abuse

Ellen, a single parent to three children, remembered her son Anthony as a bright, caring, and high-spirited little boy. He was the middle child and the one who always seemed to need the most attention. Then, in middle school, right after Ellen and her husband divorced, Anthony started acting out. He became combative with her, skipped classes, got poor grades, and picked fights with his siblings. Yet he was an angel with his father, even though they rarely saw each other after the divorce.

By the eleventh grade, Anthony was abusing prescription drugs. Ellen blamed herself because she felt she should have gotten him help after the divorce. But she was stressed and trying to manage her own mental health while providing for her three kids.

Ellen's other two children, Allyson and Justin, became productive adults, while Anthony continued to struggle. Allyson and Justin complained about how their mother always took care of Anthony and rarely celebrated them. Their experiences with their brother had been mostly negative, so they wanted nothing to do with him. He lied, instigated arguments, stole from them when they were teenagers, and most of all caused their mother a lot of stress.

Ellen often helped Anthony pay his rent, and she checked on him constantly to try to fix his problems. She wasn't there for Allyson and Justin in the same way because she felt they didn't need her. She dreamed of retiring after twenty-five years at her job, but the money lost on Anthony made her unsure if she'd be able to live how she'd planned.

Meanwhile, Anthony Sr. wasn't at all helpful. He said of his namesake, "He's grown," and took no responsibility for how the divorce had impacted his son.

Ellen believed she was responsible for Anthony because no one else would take care of him. Her biggest fear was that he would end up in jail or become homeless because of his drug use. Therefore, she tried to protect him from what she saw as an inevitable future if she didn't help. She didn't understand why Allyson and Justin complained so much about her attachment to him, and she couldn't understand why no one else cared enough to help her. In trying to save one son, she was damaging her relationship with herself and her other two children.

We Cannot Save People from Themselves

Guilt can lead parents to do more than they reasonably and appropriately can. The narrative they tell themselves is "If I had ____, this wouldn't have happened," or "If I hadn't done ____, this wouldn't have happened." The truth is, there's no way to predict the future, and there's no way to change the past. Ellen cannot know precisely what happened to Anthony psychologically during his childhood, but she assumes she's the primary cause. Therefore, she feels it's her responsibility to fix him. But Ellen cannot save her son. She can only get him support for his substance use issues.

It's sad and heartbreaking to watch a family member struggle with addiction, but it's freeing to recognize that you can't make people sober. You can only *want* them to be. Often, in families where addiction is present, all the family members feel the impact. As the famous saying goes, addiction is a family disease.

As Ellen grieved the loss of her little boy, she couldn't treat him as a man who might be capable of getting help for himself. She minimized the extent of his addiction and provided resources for him to function so that he never had to experience the consequences of his actions. Anthony may not have needed to hit rock bottom, but he did need to see how his drug use affected his life.

Definition of "Addiction"

Addiction is categorized by the inability to stop using drugs or alcohol or to stop gambling, shopping, and so on at will. When someone can't freely stop a behavior that causes life consequences, relationship and mental health issues, or the inability to function without the behavior, addiction may be an issue. While studies continue to shed new light on substance use, it's widely accepted that drugs, alcohol, gambling, and shopping addictions can be caused by brain functioning. A study from the Canadian Association for Neuroscience noted, "Dysfunction in brain regions that assign value to possible options may lead to choosing harmful behaviours." This study concluded that unhealthy patterns of decision-making cause addiction.

With alcohol and drugs, the terms "substance abuse," "disordered alcohol or drug use," and "substance misuse" are commonly being used instead of "addiction." The stigma associated with alcoholism and addiction has led people with substance abuse problems to identify with the term "substance misuse." I will use a variety of terms throughout the book, based on what I'm describing.

Drug and Alcohol Issues in Families Might Look Like:

Inability to take care of household needs or children

Example: Tabitha took care of herself in the evenings because after work, her mother started drinking heavily.

Consequences in the daily family routine

Example: Tabitha rode to school with a friend from down the street because her mother could no longer drive after getting her second DUI.

Damaged relationships

Example: Tabitha's mom was in and out of toxic dating relationships because when drunk, she argued with her partners. They would get fed up and leave after a while.

Constant physical toll

Example: Tabitha woke her mother up for work on weekdays because she was hungover and rarely heard her alarm.

Drain on financial resources

Example: Their utilities were often disconnected. At ten years old, Tabitha couldn't wait to turn fifteen so that she could start working to help with the bills.

Mental and emotional health issues

Example: Tabitha felt anxious when her mother wasn't

home because she worried that her mom might be in trouble or in danger.

Children from Homes with Drug and Alcohol Misuse Typically Experience Increased Rates of:

- Academic problems
- Challenges with intimate relationships in adulthood
- Mental health issues—primarily anxiety and depression
- Difficulty recognizing and communicating their emotions
- Secrecy, shame, and mistrust

When both parents are heavy drinkers, children usually experience worse outcomes than those who have one heavy-drinker parent. They feel the effects of both parents, leaving them with no primary adult to meet their needs.

Common Relationship Issues That Children of Addicts Experience in Adulthood:

- Questioning drinking or substance use habits even when they're normal
- Trust
- Dependency
- Control
- Expressing feelings
- Expressing needs

Gambling Addictions in Families Might Look Like:

Using the family savings to fund the habit

Example: Isaac counted on his college fund to cover his

education. When it was time to select a school, he discovered that his father had depleted his college savings.

Lying about having the gambling under control

Example: Isaac's father never admitted to having a problem with gambling despite spending long hours at the nearby casino on a regular basis.

Putting the family's safety in jeopardy because of financial debt

Example: After depleting most of his financial resources, Isaac's father began borrowing money from loan sharks.

Shopping Addictions in Families Might Look Like:

Using shopping as a way to cope with stress or significant life problems

Example: After Sharon's mother died, she began treating herself to more and more expensive shopping sprees. She rarely wore the clothes she bought, but shopping distracted her from her grief.

Living beyond one's financial means

Example: Sharon was avoiding one bill in order to be able to pay another.

Overspending as a way to cover feelings of guilt from financial problems

Example: After seeing that she couldn't pay her bills, Sharon felt so guilty that she went on another shopping binge to distract herself from the problem.

No control over spending behavior

Example: Sharon's partner complained that she needed to borrow money from him to cover her credit card bills while he paid the majority of the household expenses.

What About Other Addictions?

Is it possible to be addicted to your phone? Yes.

Is it possible to be addicted to sex? Yes.

Is it possible to be addicted to caffeine? Yes.

You can problematically misuse anything that has a detrimental effect on your life. That said, everything we do regularly isn't necessarily an addiction. For instance, if someone has an alcoholic beverage daily, it doesn't mean they're misusing alcohol. Frequency doesn't always determine if someone is addicted or not. Remember that addiction is based on an inability to shift habits, particularly when experiencing negative consequences from them. Not every vice is problematic. It's essential to know how a behavior is impacting your life and relationships, and whether you can set it aside when there's a negative impact.

Behaviors of People in the Family Who Misuse Substances

In the family at the beginning of the chapter, Anthony's substance use issues affected everyone. As a reaction to substance misuse, family members may deal with the following problems when addiction is a part of the landscape.

Defensiveness

People tend to get defensive when a problem is presented that they aren't ready to handle. They may switch topics or make nonsensical excuses. For example, "I wasn't drunk-driving. I fell asleep in my car while at a light." Defensiveness makes it hard to reason with someone whose sole objective is to deflect responsibility.

Denial

Not only can the person with the substance use issue be in denial, but so can family members. When we don't want to face something, denying that it exists gives us temporary comfort. When other family members are more vocal about the addiction, however, there is inevitable conflict. It can be particularly frustrating for them when there's blatant evidence of a problem, such as someone losing a job due to their substance use. Denial is an unhealthy coping mechanism used to maintain dysfunctional systems rather than to change them.

Blaming Others

In blaming others, people accept zero accountability for what happens in their lives. Of course, we are affected by what happens to us, but we have a choice about how we proceed in life.

When someone is defensive, blames others, or is in denial, it might sound like:

- "I didn't mean it that way."
- "You do the same thing."
- "You're too sensitive."
- "Why do you always have an issue with something?"
- "I did it, but they did, too, and you weren't mad at them."
- "That wasn't my intention."

- "You shouldn't be upset, because this isn't a big deal."
- "Stop being dramatic."

Emotional Immaturity

Chronological age and emotional age are not the same. Sometimes, people grow older without growing up or becoming wiser. People with substance abuse issues don't function in the same way as nonaddictive people in their age group. Even when they become sober, they might not mature. From children of parents who misuse substances, I've heard, "Why can't they be responsible? They're all grown up and should know better." I've found it helpful to assist them in considering the behavioral age of their parent or other childhood caregivers rather than their own biological age. A parent can be sixty-five years old with the emotional capacity of a twelve-year-old.

Selfishness

Unintentional harm is still harmful. While a person's substance use issues aren't about you, they can ultimately have a negative impact on your life. Misusing substances likely causes a person to focus more on themselves and less on the needs of the people around them. Even when they become sober, they can still have a tendency to focus on themselves. Since they've been the center of their world for a long time, they have to learn how to consider others.

Unintentional harm is still harmful.

Manipulation

To get their needs met, people with substance issues sometimes manipulate others. Guilt-tripping is a common tactic, as is withholding affection until they get what they want. They might say, "I don't have anyone else to ask," or "I need money today to keep my lights from being disconnected," or "I will come to the cookout if you help me with my rent."

Emotional Neglect

The absence of enough emotional nurturing, care, and attention is emotional neglect. Often, it's unintentional and yet very impactful. It affects us just as much to be ignored as it does to be deliberately harmed. It's a common form of childhood trauma, especially in homes with substance misuse and physical abuse. The wounds are invisible, yet many people suffer the effects of being neglected without understanding the source of their pain.

Ways That Parents Emotionally Neglect Their Kids (At Any Age)

Not being there when it matters

Kids need guidance from adults, and without it, they're left to figure things out independently or from peers who may also lack the appropriate knowledge. For example, when Kellie started her period, she was in class at school. No one had ever talked to her about what to expect or what to do. So when she saw the blood, she thought it meant she must be hurt in some way. The school called her home, but Kellie's mom simply brought her pads without explaining anything or checking in with Kellie about her feelings.

Expecting kids to be a mini version of themselves

Every child is unique, and although their caregivers influence them, kids may feel different from the rest of the family. Allowing kids to be different gives them the confidence to be authentic.

Everyone in Franklin's family had a "good job" with benefits and steady pay, while Franklin enjoyed the arts, acting, and dancing. He knew he couldn't envision his life in a career that didn't involve pursuing his passions. But whenever he mentioned dance and theater, his parents claimed they weren't a career and refused to support those endeavors.

Dismissing emotions

Kids have feelings about the adults in their lives, and they have feelings about what's happening in their lives. Ignoring a child's need for emotional support makes them think their feelings aren't valid. Studies have shown that just one adult who cares can positively impact a child's life.

When Will's parents divorced, he was twelve years old. He stayed with his mom and went from seeing his father daily to seeing him just two days per month. Will felt the weight of his father's absence, yet no one talked to him about the divorce or how he might be feeling.

In her book, *Notes from Your Therapist*, Allyson Dinneen talks about being emotionally neglected. When she was little, her mother died in a plane crash, but no one spoke to Allyson about what had happened. Life went on as if her mother had simply disappeared. But Allyson couldn't ignore it. Even when things seem hard to explain, it's imperative to have critical conversations and emotional check-ins with kids.

Requiring children to take care of themselves with no support or supervision

Kids aren't appropriate caregivers for themselves or younger children. Even when kids are left alone age-appropriately, it's healthy to provide them with instructions and expectations. Putting kids in a position to figure out too much for themselves or their young family members gives them adult responsibilities at an unreasonable age. It makes sense that parents who need support might want help from older children, but it's harmful when kids miss out on their own extracurricular activities, academics, or time being a kid.

Samantha couldn't participate in after-school activities because she had to pick up her two younger siblings. On weekends, when her mother wanted to go out, Samantha had to watch them. While she cared for her brother and sister, she resented not having a life because her mother didn't have an adult to help with them.

In dysfunctional families, "you're mature for your age" often means this:

- You know how to stay out of the way.
- You help the adults figure their way through a crisis.
- You're a people-pleaser who knows how to care for others.
- You're an emotional confidant for an adult.
- You've taken on adult duties.
- You make more sense than others around you.
- You know how to be invisible.
- You don't cause problems.
- You skipped being an age-appropriate child to take on activities of adults.

Not allowing children to show vulnerability

Humans are emotional beings, and it's normal for kids to be emotionally expressive. When upsetting things happen, they cry and scream. This isn't "bad" behavior. It's an expression of emotion—and it's the job of caring adults to help kids learn to accept and process their emotions, not suppress them to make others feel better.

At his grandmother's funeral, an older uncle told Todd, who was twelve years old, to "stop crying and be strong." Todd had just lost his grandmother, who had helped raise him.

When kids express their emotions, they should never be told to stop feeling. Of course, if a child is yelling while sad, it makes sense to redirect them to a calmer expression of their emotions. It's also helpful to name what they're feeling, while giving them a safe space to express those feelings.

Showing little or no interest in getting to know their children

Kids want to be seen by their parents, and they value being known. Some parents are emotionally immature or self-absorbed. Therefore, they may forget how to be there for others, including their children.

Leah's parents had no clue what she liked. The only thing they cared to remember was what she liked when she was a toddler. She felt that she constantly had to remind her parents of her preferences. At around thirteen years old, she stopped repeating herself and let them assume whatever they wanted.

Signs of Emotionally Immature Parents

- You feel lonely when you're with them.
- The relationship is one-sided (all about them).
- They dismiss or minimize your emotions.
- They relate in a superficial way.
- They blame you for issues they caused.
- They have highly emotional reactions.
- They avoid vulnerability.
- They demand compliance.
- They don't respect boundaries.
- They expect you to guess how they feel.
- They try to trigger you.
- They hold you accountable for their feelings.
- They make their problems seem more significant than yours.
- They are unable to hold space for your feelings or problems.
- They guilt or shame you into doing what they want.

Showing emotional distance

Expressing emotions is healthy for both kids and adults, and kids learn by observation. If the adults around them don't express their feelings, kids may not be emotionally expressive either, or they will judge themselves for emotional expression. The absence of emotion is not healthy.

Tammie never saw any of the adults in her family cry. They all seemed to hold it together so well. So she practiced what she saw, and even when she wanted to, she refused to let herself feel anything for too long.

Lacking rules or structure

Although not having rules seems appealing, it also feels very unsafe to kids. Structure is a healthy way for parents to show care for their children's health and well-being. Kids lack the knowledge to know what's best for them, so they need adults to provide rules to keep them safe.

Latoya's mom was the "cool parent" who talked about sex, not in a judgmental way but in a friend kind of way. She allowed Latoya's friends to smoke, drink, and hang out at her house, saying, "Kids should learn their limits by finding out when they've had too much." But Latoya wanted guidance, not another friend.

Parenting while distracted

Electronic devices are consuming the attention of both adults and children. Parents are often physically present with children, yet not mentally or emotionally present because they use devices instead of connecting and tuning in. Sitting around a dinner table together while everyone uses devices is hardly quality time with one another. So it's essential to maintain device use limits for both children and adults.

Most times, when Marie tried to talk to her dad about something, he was on the phone, either watching a video or browsing social media. Whenever she jumped in to ask him a question, his response was short, and he seemed agitated.

Physical Neglect

When children aren't cared for properly with food, shelter, and clothing, they're physically neglected. Eric attended school in the winter without a coat. His teacher found one in the lost and found and gave it to Eric so that he wouldn't be cold.

Physical neglect can look like:

- Not having clothing appropriate for the weather
- Not having access to electricity, gas, or water
- Not eating consistently
- Not having proper dental care
- Not having a safe place to live
- Not having a stable place to live
- Not having appropriate supervision
- Not having safety assured
- Not having physical needs addressed

Physical Abuse

Hitting or slapping children is physical abuse that may bring about legal intervention. Physical and sexual abuse leave visible scars, as well as emotional ones. This is why laws exist to protect children. However, laws aren't enough to prevent harm from being done.

Children who are physically or emotionally abused have higher incidences of:

- Death by suicide
- Eating issues
- Chronic pain
- Migraines
- Violence in adult relationships

- Addictions
- Mental health issues
- Severe PMS
- Fibroids
- Problem relationships

Emotional and Verbal Abuse

Name-calling, demeaning, bullying, and threatening are forms of verbal abuse. Using profanity to talk down to children is also verbally abusive. Even when kids are misbehaving, it's never OK to call them names or cuss them out. The tongue can be a weapon. When people are chronically abused verbally, they struggle with low self-esteem and feelings of inadequacy.

Signs of emotional and verbal abuse can include:

- The silent treatment
- Blaming others for your feelings
- Manipulating to get what you want
- Intentionally shaming someone
- Ridiculing someone for expressing emotions
- Ignoring a person when they express their feelings or thoughts
- Not responding to requests for comfort
- Telling someone how they should or should not feel
- Gaslighting (making someone question what they think)
- Ignoring attempts at communication

If you experienced emotional abuse or neglect in childhood, it's likely that you:

- Wonder if you'll ever feel normal
- Struggle to forgive your parents

- Fear setting boundaries
- Feel lonely because no one knows how you truly feel
- Search for answers about "why"
- Experience mental health issues
- Feel anxious often
- Unconsciously self-sabotage yourself
- Worry about becoming a parent
- Have issues forming secure attachments
- Feel like an imposter when life goes well
- Worry about repeating dysfunctional family patterns

Family relationships are the only type of relationship where people are expected to ignore and easily forgive abuse, neglect, and abandonment. When people remain in relationships where abuse or neglect has occurred, they often experience resentment, anger, grief, fear, and sadness. Just because the abuse or neglect is no longer present doesn't mean that the person has overcome the effects. Also, challenges remain even in adult relationships. For instance, parents who misused drugs when their children were young may still abuse drugs when their children become adults. Maintaining relationships with the perpetrators of trauma can exacerbate symptoms of depression, anxiety, post-traumatic stress disorder, bipolar disorder, and other mental health issues. Many adults struggle in their relationships with family members who harmed them as children. There's no such thing as forgetting. We can ignore, deny, or push it down, but many never forget trauma from childhood. Even when someone has no physical memory of it, their body and neurological system respond to the trauma.

There's no such thing as forgetting.

It's important to note that abuse and neglect are not economic issues. Children from affluent homes also face challenges with abuse, neglect, and addiction.

Children of people who misuse substances often think:

- "They choose drugs over me."
- "They choose alcohol over me."

Addiction is not a choice, and it's a place of powerlessness. Your parents can love you and have an issue with drugs or alcohol; addiction is not an offense to you. Your parents may love you and can't stop engaging in unhealthy behaviors. So often, children of parents with substance use issues think, "If they loved me, they would stop." The truth is, the inability to stop is what characterizes an addict—they can't.

Once you start to understand that their behavior is not against you, you begin to see them struggling with something they cannot control. Working through your issues with your parents requires that you humanize their experiences. They didn't stop because they couldn't, or they haven't quit because they can't. You are enough, and someone's addiction, even your parents', impacts you, but it's not your fault, and it isn't about you.

EXERCISE

Grab your journal or a piece of paper to complete the following prompts:

- ❊ How has substance misuse impacted your family?
- ❊ Have you maintained a relationship with a family member who harmed you in childhood?
- ❊ In your family, have issues from your childhood been addressed with the person who caused them?

CHAPTER 4

Repeating the Cycle

Denise was raised by her grandmother. Her relationship with her mom was more like they were siblings who had been raised years apart. At six months old, Denise went to live with her grandmother because her mother couldn't care for her while also working and living her life.

Ten years later, her mother married and had four more children, one of whom ended up living with her grandmother. Each of the children had their own relationship style with their mother, but none of them had a parent-child relationship with her.

At no point did Denise's mother attempt to retrieve her from her grandmother's house. As far as her grandmother was concerned, Denise was her own daughter, and that was the way she planned to keep it. Denise's father wasn't in her life either.

Her mother and her grandmother had both been raised by grandparents, so in their family this was customary, especially when the parent was unmarried. Her grandmother was even described as "wild" in her younger years; she calmed down and became financially stable only as she got older and got married. Because she didn't raise her own children, she believed it was her duty to step up for Denise's mother by raising the grandchildren. She was able to give her grandchildren a life their mother could not.

When Denise reached adulthood, her mother wanted a closer

relationship, but it was hard for Denise to build a relationship with someone who had been so distant by choice most of her life. Denise's mother
never seemed to mind not parenting her own children, but Denise couldn't
justify her mother's absence. Her mother wasn't addicted to drugs or anything, so Denise wondered why she didn't raise her own kids. The more her
mother tried to be a part of Denise's life, the more Denise resented it. Her
mother couldn't understand Denise's feelings, because, despite some rocky
times, Denise's grandmother and mother now had a healthy relationship.

Why People Repeat Unhealthy Family Patterns

In the beginning of my career, I saw a mother and teenage daughter in my
first family therapy sessions. The uncle, the mother's brother, was molest-
ing the daughter, and the mother revealed that he had molested her as well
when she was a teen. As I watched the mother connect with the reality of
a dysfunctional pattern of behaviors, my heart ached for her because it
wasn't a cycle anyone would want to repeat.

People aren't always aware that a pattern exists, but when they are, the
patterns are often regarded as deep family secrets. Some families hope
that a dysfunctional situation is simply an anomaly, and perhaps it will
disappear if it isn't addressed. But changes don't happen unless the problem is remedied.

Some things don't get better with time. A hard thing that isn't talked
about enough is not having the love you needed in childhood and accepting that the adults in question still aren't what you need today. Even
though we can't change people, it can be deeply tempting to try—and it
can feel like the repair work we need, when in fact it is not our work to do.
Give yourself a lot of grace if you're still accepting that someone important
in your early life is still unable to give you what you need.

Ignorance is bliss because it absolves us of the need to change. Some-times, it's easier to pretend to be unaware of the truth because we don't want to do the hard work of dealing with conflict and ugly realities within the family. Family patterns of unhealthy behav-iors can perpetuate for years due to a fear of isolation, a contentment with the status quo, or a lack of the tools needed to change.

> *Ignorance is bliss because it absolves us of the need to change.*

Fear of Isolation

Naturally, we humans desire to belong, and being pushed out of our family is difficult for most of us to accept. Deciding to break a family pattern can and does cause issues in our relationships with family. Even when behav-iors are blatantly wrong, it can be challenging for the offending family members to accept the harm they've caused. When someone brings family dysfunction out into the open, there's a chance that others in the family will try to deny the problem.

It's brave to speak out against unhealthy patterns. Unfortunately, the potentially devastating impact of being vocal keeps many people silent.

Content with the Way of Being

Some people may not see anything wrong with specific family issues. For instance, gossiping about family members could be an acceptable norm within a family. Gossiping might even be joked about or downplayed. However, even when people are content with certain behaviors, it doesn't mean those behaviors are healthy. It just means that no one has the neces-sary tools to change the patterns.

What you might notice as a problem might be an acceptable way of being for someone else. We don't universally agree about problems. You can't persuade or convince people to change even if you can see how changing could improve their life. You can see how not changing impacts their life and how their behaviors affect you. But the only thing you can change is you. So in some families, it might feel better to live with the dysfunction than to do anything about it.

Lacking the Tools to Start

Without proper role models or support, it's hard to know where or how to start. Perhaps you see a problem, but trying to solve it can be just as anxiety-provoking as being in the middle of the problem itself.

The ways we show up in family relationships tend to be habitual. So out of habit, you might invite certain family members to gatherings. If you decide to shift your invitation list, others in the family might question you about it. Family relationships are interconnected, so when you decide to change the nature of one relationship, it might change other relationships in the family as well. For instance, if you decide to stop speaking to your sibling, your parents might change the way they engage with you. Indeed, it can be hard to start changing patterns because your choices impact everyone.

How to Handle Current Abuse in the Family

If there is a sexual perpetrator in your family, you can't ignore their behavior. In too many families, children are thrust into the midst of people who have harmed other family members. We can't assume that a perpetrator will eventually become a safe person to have around children.

In my sixteen years as a therapist, I've heard many stories of people informing their parents of abuse by family members, only to have their parents and other adults continue their relationships with the abusive person. This makes the child feel unsafe within the family, leaving them emotionally neglected.

Instead of telling your kids, "Stay away from ____ [insert predator's name]," keep your kids away from people who aren't safe. Children aren't responsible for protecting themselves against known family perpetrators. It isn't their responsibility to manage their relationships with people who can potentially harm them. Adults who are harmful should never have access to your children.

Obviously, if a family member is harming a child, something legally should be done to protect that child and other children from potentially being harmed. Once we're adults, however, it's our responsibility to protect ourselves. So only you can decide how you want to change to handle the situation. As an adult, you may choose to call out your abuser to the family, seek legal action, or avoid the person whose behaviors are problematic for you.

Unhealed Trauma Affects Adult Relationships

It isn't uncommon for people from dysfunctional families to have issues in many of their adult relationships.

Common issues for people from dysfunctional families include

- Trust issues (self and others)
- Dependency issues (counterdependency and codependency)
- Control issues
- Emotional disconnection (called "alexithymia")
- Challenges with expressing needs

Trust Issues (Self and Others)

Jonathan's mother was critical of his every move. He never seemed to do things well enough for her. She always found a flaw or had an example of how he could have done better. Despite the fact that he was on the honor roll throughout school, Jonathan's mother demanded more. In college, he became paralyzed when he had to make decisions independently. He was always afraid he wasn't doing something correctly. He didn't trust himself to be good enough despite the proof that he was doing a great job.

People you trust can

- Harm you
- Betray you
- Hurt your feelings
- Take advantage of you
- Misguide you
- Abuse you
- Be jealous of you
- Blame you
- Not support you
- Gossip about you
- Steal from you
- Use your words against you

Without a doubt, if you've been harmed by a family member, that can be the source of trust issues you may have with others from childhood through adulthood if your issues aren't acknowledged, processed, and healed.

Dependency Issues (Counterdependency and Codependency)

Cecelia's parents always seemed preoccupied with their careers. As the only child, she was taught from a young age to take care of herself. She was so attached to the mindset of figuring things out on her own that even when people offered to help, she declined. She denied her need for help for so long that she genuinely believed she could do everything independently.

Cecelia felt lonely and knew that being counterdependent led to her not having anyone to lean on when she needed it.

In dysfunctional families, dependency issues typically swing in one direction or the other. Counterdependency is the denial of personal need, while codependency is when you help someone avoid consequences, saving them from unpleasant experiences. Neither option is helpful, as healthy giving and receiving lie somewhere in the middle.

Control Issues

Justina's homelife was unpredictable because her father couldn't keep a job. Her mother was no longer there, so he was the sole parent. Her father received assistance from Justina's grandmother when the utilities were disconnected or when they needed groceries. Justina vowed to herself that she would be able to take care of all her financial needs without ever needing anyone to support her when she became an adult. So now, she seeks to stay in control. Whenever she dates someone, she tries to control various aspects of their life, especially how they spend their money.

Safety is an essential need. When we feel that our safety is threatened, it's understandable to try to control our environment. When we have an area of sensitivity, such as around finances, we're likely hypersensitive about those issues. Although seeking to control seems like the best action for staying safe, it can actually be counterproductive, especially when there's no real threat and only a need to ensure that everything is positive and predictable in the future.

Signs That You're Trying to Control Someone
- Pushing them to think and be like you
- Managing areas of their life that have no impact on you (not minding your business)
- Determining what they can or can't do with their life

- Demanding that they change for you
- Manipulating them into changing their behavior
- Creating rules for how they "should" do things in their life
- Telling them what's best for them

Emotional Disconnection (Alexithymia)

"You shouldn't feel that way." "What do you have to cry about?" Andrew often heard these statements from his parents. At forty years old, he was in the process of getting divorced for the second time. His soon-to-be ex-wife told him she never knew what he was feeling because he never communicated his emotions to her. He had to agree because he realized he didn't know what he was feeling himself.

He did know he didn't want his marriage to end, but he wasn't sure how to be more emotional, as his wife requested. Emotional disconnection usually leads to divorce because the partner who isn't disconnected feels isolated and lonely in the relationship.

An inability to identify and express emotions is called alexithymia. "I don't know what I feel" is a typical refrain from people who have this condition. Even when they know what they feel, it's challenging for them to express their feelings to others. In families where emotional expression is discouraged, people can disconnect over time from their feelings, and therefore can't or won't express what they feel.

Six Ways to Manage Alexithymia

1. Use a feelings chart—yes, the one with faces—to figure out what you feel.
2. Use a mood tracker to assess what you're feeling throughout the day.
3. Practice journaling about feelings. Pick an emotion and write about a time when you've experienced it.

4. Take steps toward using feeling words in everyday conversation. This might be awkward at first, but it will become more natural with practice.

5. Pay attention to how other people express emotions and ask them questions about their feelings.

6. Therapy can be a place where you learn to identify, connect to, and process your emotions.

Challenges with Expressing Needs

Evelyn's parents were older, and when she was a kid, her siblings were already adults. Her parents challenged her to figure things out on her own, so that was what she did. Even when she needed help, she tried to figure it out because she didn't want to bother anyone. After she broke her ankle, she needed help completing basic tasks like getting into the shower and moving around her house. Evelyn was stuck trying to take care of herself because she didn't want to ask for the help she needed.

Humans are needy, and being needy isn't always a bad thing. Of course, we don't want to burden others, so it can be tough to ask for help when we've been told to "figure it out." No matter what you've been told, however, you can't figure everything out on your own. You have needs, and it's OK to admit that you do. Denying your needs doesn't make them go away; it just leaves them unmet.

In a poll on Instagram, I asked, "What family patterns do you want to break?"

These were the top twenty responses (in no particular order):

- Alcoholism
- Codependency
- Keeping secrets
- Staying in dysfunctional relationships

- Counterdependency
- Gossiping about family members
- Verbal abuse
- Emotional disconnection
- Gaslighting
- Ignoring major problems
- Fat shaming
- Financial instability
- Keeping up appearances to the outside world
- Enmeshment
- Emotional immaturity
- Lack of boundaries
- Emotional neglect
- Passive-aggressiveness
- People-pleasing
- Beating children

Numerous things from this list are present in some families, but even one thing can impact how you function in your adult relationships.

How Childhood Issues Impact Romantic Relationships

Harville Hendrix, Ph.D., and Helen LaKelly Hunt, Ph.D., developed imago therapy to help couples deal with how childhood wounds affect their ability to connect with their partner. Having a partner with childhood wounds can lead to unrealistic expectations in relationships. The issues that people experience with their partners are usually the same issues that first presented in their childhood. Therefore, the emotional intensity is heightened as they attempt to work through these issues with their partner.

For example, Derrick was abandoned by his mother when he was a child. As an adult, he unconsciously sabotaged his romantic relationships by cheating and withholding affection. Forming attachments and allowing himself to be vulnerable scared Derrick because he feared being left. He found it safer to engage without creating deep connections with others.

Your partner can't heal your deep wounds left by childhood trauma, but they can help you facilitate your healing. Conversely, some partners trigger trauma wounds by re-creating familiar traumatic experiences. For example, if you grew up in a home with parents who gave you the silent treatment when they were upset, this might trigger feelings of abandonment in you when your partner does something similar. To break the cycle, it's important to practice awareness of what childhood issues resurface in your adult romantic relationships.

Grandfamilies

Families headed by grandparents rather than parents are referred to as "grandfamilies." In the United States, 2.5 million children are raised by grandparents, usually because their adult children have challenges with misusing substances, inadequate housing, and other social issues, or they are in the military service.

Grandparents, aunts, uncles, and other family members can be loving and supportive, but they can't replace the role of a biological parent. Even when your parents aren't a part of your life, the role of a parent to a child is clear. The absence of a biological parent from a child's life causes the child to wonder how to exist with such a deep loss. Even when children are placed in the healthiest situations with family or adoptive parents for their own well-being, they may still long to know or have a relationship with their biological parents.

There's a unique difference between raising a child's grandchild and helping a grandchild who needs additional support.

Raising a grandchild can look like:

- Being responsible for medical care
- Handling all decision-making
- Providing a safe environment for kids
- Supporting a child financially
- Setting expectations for grandchildren

Supporting a grandchild can look like:

- Providing supplemental childcare when needed
- Being present at extracurricular activities
- Buying gifts
- Offering guidance when needed or asked
- Upholding the expectations set by parents

Often, kinship care is a better alternative than foster care. Children are wired to attach to their parents. At the height of the COVID-19 pandemic, there was grave concern about children raised by older adults, the population most at risk of contracting and being hospitalized for COVID-19. Support increases a child's well-being, so grandparents can be a healthy addition to a child's life. However, when the parents are absent, children often struggle with issues of abandonment. Typically, grandparents raising children are more prone to health issues, depression, and limited resources due to a fixed income.

What Happened to You?

Awareness is what saves us from repeating patterns. Understanding your story is a process that unfolds over time, and your story is constantly evolving. Well into adulthood, I watched a Lifetime network movie that caused me to recall a traumatic event in my life. The movie was about teen dating violence, and I remembered witnessing a family member being hit with a car by a boyfriend when they were teenagers. I couldn't believe how clearly the memory

Awareness is what saves us from repeating patterns.

popped into my head. That event shaped me in ways that I hadn't yet realized. I'm particularly sensitive when someone raises their voice even the slightest bit. What is your story?

EXERCISE

Grab your journal or a piece of paper to complete the following prompts:

* ❋ What patterns have you repeated? Use the list from my Instagram poll (see "Challenges with Expressing Needs" on page 57) for ideas.
* ❋ What patterns do you want to break?
* ❋ Consider an experience when you found it challenging to verbalize your feelings.

CHAPTER 5

Trauma Across Generations

Donald came from a long line of alcoholics—his grandfather, father, multiple uncles, and now himself. He had his first drink when he was just twelve years old. Being drunk was the only way Donald knew how to feel at ease and forget about the problems in his house. His family was so consumed in their own chaos that no one noticed until he was drinking daily by age seventeen.

Donald had always found it difficult to connect with his father until they became drinking buddies. Suddenly, they bonded over their shared interest.

After Donald's second wife threatened to leave him if he didn't get help, he started couples therapy with her. Unfortunately, he disagreed with his wife that he had a problem. He considered himself a "functional" drinker who financially took care of his responsibilities and drank only in the evenings and on weekends. He wasn't drunk all the time, like his father, or unemployed, like his uncles.

Donald was under the impression that he could stop whenever he wanted, but he didn't want to stop yet, even though it was causing problems for his family. His free time was spent drinking at his father's house or with his friends. In our sessions, he seemed to love his wife and the child they shared, but he found it hard to release his constant companion—alcohol.

It wasn't until his wife made good on her threats and left their home with their child that Donald seriously started to explore his history and relationship with alcohol.

He asked himself the following questions:

- How is alcohol impacting my life?
- What is my family history with alcohol misuse?
- What constitutes a problem with alcohol?
- Can I change my behavior with alcohol on my own, or will I need support?
- How is alcohol helping me cope?

Sometimes the Apple Doesn't Fall Far from the Tree

In *Depression Is Contagious: How the Most Common Mood Disorder Is Spreading Around the World and How to Stop It*, Michael D. Yapko, Ph.D., notes that children of depressed parents are three times more likely to develop depression themselves. Parents are models for their children, and children pick up on both their positive and negative qualities. When parents are preoccupied with managing the issues in their lives, they often leave their children to figure things out for themselves with little to no guidance. Many children with distracted parents suffer from chronic feelings of loneliness. For Donald, the only way to connect with his father was through drinking.

Early in my career, I provided therapy to children and parents in the foster care system. The severity of abuse and parental compliance toward treatment determined whether children returned home or remained in foster care. On average, 39 percent of children removed from their homes have families with drug and alcohol problems. In many instances, the parent's substance misuse issues are coupled with a history of trauma and untreated mental health problems, predominantly post-traumatic stress disorder (PTSD) and depression. People with symptoms of PTSD are three times more likely to abuse substances, and one-third of people with symptoms of depression are likely to misuse substances. Therapists working to help people with substance use disorders often treat family, coping, trauma, and mental health problems. Children who grow up with parents who misuse substances often learn it as a coping strategy. In dysfunctional homes, chaos is frequently managed by misusing substances to numb or ignore emotional pain.

Clinical Criteria for Substance Use Disorders

Substance use disorders are diagnosed by meeting two of the following characteristics within a twelve-month period:

1. Taking substances in larger quantities than intended or deemed safe
2. Desire to cut down but inability to do so
3. Spending large amounts of time to acquire, use, or recover from substance use
4. Uncontrollable craving or urges to use
5. Inability to function at home, school, or work due to misuse
6. Persistent problematic use even after consequences
7. Reducing or abandoning healthy recreational, work, or social activities due to misuse
8. Putting self and others in danger to acquire substances
9. Using despite cognitive or psychological problems due to the substance

10. Using substances in larger quantities to achieve desired effect
11. Withdrawal symptoms are present and can be relieved only by using the substance

Based on this criteria, from the fifth edition of *The Diagnostic and Statistical Manual of Mental Disorders*, a diagnosis can vary from mild, with two or three symptoms; moderate, with four or five symptoms; or severe, with six or more symptoms.

Parents who haven't dealt with their own family trauma often intentionally or unintentionally inflict trauma on their children. An absence of awareness is a breeding ground for cycles to repeat. Both genetic and environmental influences can increase the likelihood of substance use and mental health issues.

> *An absence of awareness is a breeding ground for cycles to repeat.*

What Is Generational Trauma?

The descendants of Holocaust survivors have been found to experience higher levels of stress-inducing hormones. When trauma isn't addressed, its rippling effect can be felt from generation to generation. Repeated unhealthy behaviors and maladaptive coping skills can manifest from generational trauma.

People who have experienced trauma often have higher reactivity toward stress. This isn't necessarily biological, as it can be environmental, learned, and modeled. Anyone is susceptible to generational trauma, however, and families that experience racial disparities, abuse, or neglect are at higher risk.

Generational trauma can present as PTSD-type symptoms such as hypervigilance, anxiety, panic, mood swings, and depression. Parents who experienced severe childhood trauma have an increased likelihood of having children with behavioral issues. Epigenetics is the study of changes in gene expression. Autoimmune and other chronic illnesses have been linked to generational trauma as well. Recent studies explore how epigenetics leaves a genetic imprint on trauma survivors and is passed down through generations.

Situations That Can Lead to Generational Trauma

- Emotional or physical neglect
- Sexual or physical abuse
- Parentification (being a little adult)
- Frequently relocating
- Growing up with parents who were addicts
- Not being raised by one or both parents
- Domestic violence
- Living in an unsafe neighborhood
- Financial insecurity
- Toxic co-parenting

"Post Traumatic Slave Syndrome" (PTSS) is a theory developed by Dr. Joy DeGruy to describe the impact of slavery on descendants of slaves. DeGruy, the author of *Post Traumatic Slave Syndrome: America's Legacy of Enduring Injury and Healing*, asserts that PTSS is a result of unresolved post-traumatic stress disorder arising from the experience of slavery transmitted across generations down to the present day, along with the stress of contemporary racial prejudice (e.g., via racial microaggressions). This manifests as a psychological, spiritual, emotional, and behavioral syndrome that results in a lack of self-esteem, persistent feelings of anger, and internalized racist beliefs.

How Trauma Can Show Up in Future Generations

- Substance use issues
- Risky sexual behaviors
- Shame
- Dysfunctional family patterns
- Domestic violence
- Unhealthy relationships
- Self-sabotage
- Sleep issues
- Unhealthy boundaries
- Mental health issues
- Codependency
- Emotional health issues
- Disordered eating

Common Generational Patterns of Dysfunction

Verbal Abuse

Lori hated going to her cousin's house for family dinners because her cousin talked about her adult children as if they weren't hers. She called them lazy and stupid, and she often had screaming matches with them. Lori found it unsettling how no one jumped in to stop the fights. Lori witnessed her grandmother and aunts saying mean things about their children.

Backstabbing

Tonya's mother and aunt hated each other, but Tonya hoped it would be different with her sister. Unfortunately, Tonya's sister was unkind and tried to sabotage Tonya's relationship with other family members. Their mother often noted how their relationship reminded her of her relationship with her own sister.

Gossiping

At the Davis family gathering, as soon as someone was out of sight, it was the norm to comment on their weight, relationship status, or anything that could be criticized. Talking disparagingly about others was so common that it was an expected part of the family conversation. When Tanisha refused to talk with a group of cousins about her brother's recent stint in jail, the tone became awkward. She recalls her mother oversharing and judging the actions of family members alongside other family members.

Difficulty Expressing Emotions

Jane never heard her father say "I love you." Her grandmother was a complex woman, and Jane was kept away from her during most of her childhood. Jane could only imagine how her grandmother was as a mother to her father.

Other Ways Generational Trauma Affects Families

- Addiction
- Single-parent homes
- Poor coping skills
- Chronic health issues
- Mother-daughter relationship issues
- Father-son relationship issues
- Sibling relationship issues
- Sexual, physical, or emotional abuse or neglect

The Cycle Continues

Generational cycles are problems experienced by multiple family members across generations. You may have seen your aunts, uncles, and cousins mimicking the same unhealthy family patterns as their elders. A popular saying, "You can't give what you didn't get," explains how some parents may struggle to overcome generational patterns. However, you *can* learn and implement new practices with education, insight, and tools. Since new parents aren't given a handbook, they may struggle to learn the skills. Some parents genuinely lack the tools to nurture and support their children. Although caring for a child is often described as "common sense," that kind of common sense is far from typical.

In most bookstores, you'll find at least one aisle filled with parenting books. Parents need tools and coping strategies to manage the demands of the job. Without the proper tools, some will mimic what they know and repeat the dysfunctional patterns of their parents. A woman once told me that she put sugar in her spaghetti sauce. When I asked why, she said that's what her mother did. When the client asked her mother about it, she found out it came from her grandmother. No one knew why. I later mentioned to her that sugar cuts the acid in the tomatoes, which is why people typically add it. But it just goes to show that unless we question whether behaviors make sense, we might perpetuate them to the detriment of everyone in our family. Adding sugar has a purpose, but some of the things we may choose to mimic have no purpose at all.

Minimization and Denial

All too often, families cope with generational trauma by minimizing or denying it. Commonly, unhealthy coping skills are used as a way to move on from trauma. But ignoring pain not only increases problems in the present generation but also sets the stage for destructive patterns in future generations.

Minimizing can sound like:

"It wasn't that bad."
"Everyone experienced something similar."
"It didn't affect us."
"Things happen."
"We have to be strong and move on."
"Leave the past in the past."
"Yesterday's problems aren't today's worries."

Denial can sound like:

"Nothing happened."
"We don't talk about that."
"I don't want to talk about it."
"I don't remember" (as a way to deflect).

Overcoming Shame

Shame is the most common reason for denying and minimizing. It keeps people silent because they believe that what happened is a reflection of who they are, so they find it embarrassing to talk through stories of abuse, neglect, and other traumas. The more families speak up, however, the more they heal. The critical difference between guilt and shame is that shame is the belief "I am bad," and guilt is the belief "I am doing something bad." People who experience shame are often subjected to mistreatment because they intuit that other people know how "bad" they are and believe that they deserve mistreatment.

If you feel shame, it impacts the way you feel about yourself and how you engage with the world. You might feel a heightened sense of anxiety when life goes well, believing that your family secrets might be uncovered, or you may worry that others won't understand your story.

AN AFFIRMATION FOR OVERCOMING SHAME

I am *not* a product of my environment. I am a product of the choices I make right now. Sometimes, those choices are influenced by my environment. However, I have a choice in deciding who I want to be. I can be different from my environment. This will not be easy, but I can do it.

EXERCISE

Grab your journal or a piece of paper to complete the following prompts:

* What family secrets have you ignored or minimized?
* Name how you've been affected by generational trauma.
* Have you ever experienced shame about your family history?

PART TWO

HEALING

CHAPTER 6

Resisting the Urge to Operate
in Dysfunction

Kelly had a tumultuous relationship with her brother Jeff. He had a slicing way with words, he had a history of manipulating their entire family to get what he wanted, and he acted entitled. Their other two siblings no longer had a relationship with him, and even refused to show up at Kelly's home if Jeff was there. But Kelly hung on because she felt she was the only person he had. Despite being burned by her brother over and over, Kelly continued the relationship, hoping that he would change.

In therapy, she explored how terrible she felt about the thought of cutting Jeff out of her life, even though she knew that he was mistreating her and that ending the relationship would be better for her. She had already tried suggesting to him that he think about how his behavior was the cause of his difficulties, but he refused to see that it wasn't always the other person's fault. Whenever she disagreed with him, he became verbally aggressive and stonewalled her.

Kelly and Jeff were close in age and used to have a lot in common, but that was no longer the case in adulthood. They'd grown up without a father, so she wondered if that accounted for Jeff's behavior. He hadn't been the best student, and he struggled to stay employed.

She envied her siblings' ability to let go of the relationship, and she acknowledged that if Jeff weren't her brother, she wouldn't have a relationship with him. But despite cringing when he called to bully and manipulate her, Kelly couldn't get over her guilt.

Change Is Hard, and Worth It

It often feels easier to go with the flow—but it keeps you stuck. Knowing there's a problem is the tip of the iceberg and might still mean you have a long road ahead. Change typically happens when you get tired enough to start doing something different. Feeling frustrated, upset, or exhausted in a relationship doesn't necessarily mean you're going to change. It simply means that you're feeling something.

Changing the dynamics of a relationship is similar to the process of breaking a habit. For Kelly, here's what this might look like:

- Letting Jeff's call go to voicemail and returning it when she's prepared to engage in the conversation
- Telling Jeff that she understands his issues with others, and she'd like them to talk about other topics
- Shifting the belief that she's the only person who can support Jeff
- Allowing Jeff to manage his issues without offering solutions
- Letting Jeff know what topics are off-limits, such as rants about siblings or parents

Instead of building more tolerance for others, perhaps it's time to change the things you no longer want to tolerate. People in my community often ask me about building their tolerance for unwanted behaviors. It typically sounds like this:

> "How do I deal with my mother being jealous of me? Whenever I
>   share good news, she offers a backhanded compliment."
> "How do I deal with my sister treating me like a child?"
> "How do I deal with my father showing up drunk to family
>   events?"

Whenever I hear "deal with," I know they're trying hard to tolerate something intolerable. Trying to handle unhealthy behaviors builds resentment, not patience. You can't, ever, and in any way, change other people, so many of us will choose to go with the flow because it seems easier than changing ourselves.

Trying to handle unhealthy behaviors builds resentment, not patience.

Stages of Change

When people enter therapy, it's typically at the pre-contemplation stage. They can feel the effects of lingering issues in their life but struggle to find the cause. People often experience anxiety, depression, and other mental health issues without understanding what lies beneath their clinical symptoms.

After studying the change process within dysfunctional family relationships, psychologists James Prochaska and Carlo DiClemente created a model for how people become ready to break a long-standing pattern. I've adapted that model here.

STAGES OF CHANGE

MAINTENANCE
- Consistent with changes
- Your feelings are no longer guiding what you allow

ACTION
- Vocal about needs
- Changing what you can on your end, not trying to change the other person

PREPARATION
- Exploring minor changes
- Inconsistent with changes
- Trying to convince the other person to change
- More verbal about issues

CONTEMPLATION
- Considering the value of changes
- Mixed emotions
- Guilt

PRE-CONTEMPLATION
- Unconscious of problems
- Covering up problems
- Making excuses

Pre-contemplation

In the pre-contemplation stage of change, we typically lack conscious awareness of the problem. However, there are indicators that a problem is present. It's common to feel resentful, hopeless, and powerless at this stage, along with denying and making excuses, because people often feel hopeless or resigned about their situation.

Indicators of pre-contemplation in families might look like:

Expecting people to be different despite the fact that nothing
  has changed with them or with us
Giving people second, third, and fourth chances to be
  something different
Repeating ourselves over and over in hopes that the other
  person will catch on

Pre-contemplation might sound like:

"I feel taken advantage of by my brother, but that's how he's
  always been."
"My parents can't handle the 'real' me; they can only see what
  they want."
"My sister is always treating me like a baby. She can't grasp the
  fact that I've grown up."
"I need to figure out a better way to deal with my grandmother's
  critical comments. She doesn't mean anything by them."

Contemplation

In this stage, awareness is building. We are beginning to see things as they are. We now consciously know what the problem is, leading to conflicting feelings such as ambivalence, guilt, shame, and regret. We begin to explore the potential benefits of change—how things could be better for the relationship, the person in question, and ourselves.

When we're in a dysfunctional relationship, everyone might not agree about what behaviors are unhealthy. Denial is sometimes the only way people know how to keep life moving along. Ignoring a problem as a way to keep peace in the family is an unfortunate norm. Awareness, on the

other hand, can be scary because it forces us to look at situations differently and feel compelled to change.

Ten Reasons You Might Choose to Stay in Unhealthy Relationships
1. You're waiting for the "good times" to reappear.
2. You're holding out hope that the other person will change.
3. You can't imagine life without the other person.
4. You don't have the financial means to leave.
5. You believe that loyalty means staying no matter what.
6. You don't think they can manage without you.
7. You fear making the wrong decision.
8. You are waiting for the other person to end the relationship.
9. You don't want to hurt other people who might be impacted.
10. You aren't tired enough.

Many clients enter the therapy relationship in the contemplation stage,
and quite often, people leave therapy in the contemplation stage. Considering change is more accessible than actually making changes, especially
changes in our families. In therapy, contemplation can last for years. This
might seem like a disappointing reality, but therapists have come to accept
that it's where we have to sit with clients until they're ready to take action.

In my early years as a therapist, I took it personally when clients were
stuck. Now I know that this is the place where many of us reside—stuck.
I'm here to help you get unstuck.

With family, ambivalence can indeed hold you back from making
healthy changes that will benefit you and the entire system.

Contemplation might sound like:

"My brother is entitled."
"My parents love me, and they need to know who I am."

"I'm not a baby anymore."

"My grandmother's words are hurtful."

If you feel stuck in the contemplation stage, consider this:

- How might change be beneficial to your mental and emotional health?
- What are you giving up to stay the same?
- Who benefits if you don't make any changes?
- How are you harming yourself by denying your needs?

Preparation

In this stage, you'll begin to experiment with minor modifications. For example, instead of allowing your brother to joke about the time you wet the bed at a friend's house, you'll say something like, "Please stop joking about that incident. It's embarrassing, not funny." Consistency might be lacking, however, as you begin to change your role in the relationship and what you allow from the others involved. Change is hard, yet it can be good for you.

In this stage, it's normal to start reading more about the issue, seeing a therapist, and processing your experiences with friends and supportive family members. All of these are good ways to validate your experiences and increase your energy to power through complex changes. You may become more vocal about your issues and encourage others to change so that you don't have to be the one doing all the work. (Again, you can't change anyone else, but you can encourage them to change themselves.)

Preparation might sound like:

"When my brother demands that I loan him money, I will give
him a time frame to pay me back. If he doesn't pay me back

on time, I won't loan him more money until his previous
debt is paid off."

"When my parents compare me with who I was as a child, I will
ask them to be present by acknowledging that this is who
I am now."

"When my sister attempts to give me unsolicited advice, I
will tell her that I'd like her to listen instead of tell me what
to do."

"When my grandmother comments about my weight gain, I will
tell her to stop."

Action

At this stage, you no longer just make statements about what you'd like to
change. You have accepted that it's your job to change your life even when
other people won't change. Your attitude has moved from thinking to doing and from victim to powerful force, and you become more assertive and
consistent with the changes you're making. At this stage, you will need
support to help you clarify your thoughts, process your emotions, and
stick to the changes.

Action might sound like:

"I'm not allowing my brother to take advantage of me."
"I am myself with my parents."
"I'm acting like an adult in my relationship with my sister."
"I'm not allowing my grandmother to demean me."

Maintenance

In this stage, you've reached the upper room of change, and you're commit-
ted to choosing a healthy relationship. You might still feel some

discomfort, such as guilt, shame, and ambivalence, but you don't allow the discomfort to stop you from choosing yourself. You're aware of the temptation to slide back into old patterns in your relationships, but you've learned how to overcome the temptation by consistently practicing changed behavior.

By practicing new behaviors over and over, you've changed your habit of dysfunction in a dysfunctional family. Of course, your work evolves and isn't ever done, because change is continuous.

Even though you've changed, from time to time you might revisit your former thoughts or former behaviors. When that happens, greet yourself in the present with grace and understanding. It's hard to overcome patterns, and it's challenging to avoid lapsing into old behaviors. Know that you might not always get it right.

Kelly, for example, is in the contemplation stage in her relationship with her brother Jeff, while her two other siblings are in the maintenance stage.

There's no set time frame for moving through the stages, and some of us will remain at a particular stage. Kelly has expressed the following concerns:

- "What will other people think?"
- "Who else will help if not me?"
- "He's my brother, and I can't stop talking to him."

What Will Other People Think?

It's common to remain in situations you don't like because of the fear of what others may think. Some societies and cultures normalize the acceptance of poor treatment from family. Therefore, telling some people about your decision might be a painful process, and there's undoubtedly fear that despite making a healthy choice, it might be unacceptable to some of them.

When people judge your relationships with your family members, they speak from their own experiences, which might be different from yours. Everyone sees family norms through a lens of their own upbringing, along with the views and beliefs they've developed through their own process of learning and growth.

Who Else Will Help If Not Me?

If you assume you're the only support that a person has, you will likely remain the only support. People are responsible for building their own support systems, and by doing everything for them, you might be getting in the way of that.

Remember This: Stepping back can be a fantastic way to allow others to show up for the person you're oversupporting and for them to begin to show up for themselves.

He's My Brother, and I Can't Stop Talking to Him.

You can love people and refuse to accept mistreatment from them regardless of their position in your life. Siblings, parents, aunts, uncles, grandparents, and cousins don't have special privileges to treat you poorly.

Remember This: Mistreatment isn't healthy behavior, no matter what role a person plays in your life.

You Get to Decide Who You Want to Be as an Adult

When I was a kid, I was a fan of soap operas. Peabo Bryson sang the intro for the show *One Life to Live*, singing, "'Cause we only have one life to live!"

It's true. You only have one life to live, and you—and only you—have to be pleased with how you live it.

As an adult, you decide:

Where you work
Who you partner with
What you eat
Who you allow to visit your home
How you spend your time
How you want to parent your child
Who you allow in your life

My biggest gripe about being a child was having to ask for permission. It burned me up to say, "Can I go to the movies?" I couldn't wait until the day I could go to the movies without asking or could say no to visiting a particular relative. Choice is freedom. With family, it might seem like you don't have a choice, but you do. Of course, sometimes the choices you make are hard. But even inaction is a choice, though a passive one. As an adult, you choose what type of life and relationships you want. You are with yourself all day and every day. The person with whom *Choice is freedom.* you spend the most time in your entire life is you.

If you decide to spend time with family, and you have a complicated relationship with them, remember this:

- You can accept people as they are and not tolerate unhealthy behaviors.
- You have a choice in how much and for how long you interact with people.
- You can decide what topics are off-limits.

- You can shut down any comments about off-limits topics.
- You don't have to engage in heated dialogue, arguments, or gossip.

Don't Allow Fear to Be Your Guiding Force

"I don't want kids, because I don't want them to be screwed up like I am," Trisha said. Her mother, Doris, terrorized her throughout childhood, and she feared doing the same to her own children. So she decided not to have any.

People commonly remain stuck in unhealthy patterns due to fear of the unknown, the things they can't control, and the what-ifs that plague them. Awareness is protection from repeating cycles, but how about if we consider positive what-ifs instead of negative ones?

Negative What-Ifs
"If I have children, I might treat them as badly as my mother
   treated me."
"If I tell my mom to stop talking to me about her issues with my
   aunt, she'll be mad."
"If I stop going to family dinners on Sundays, they'll think I'm
   acting funny."

Positive What-Ifs
"If I have children, I can stop the cycle of abuse."
"If I tell my mother to stop talking to me about her issues with
   my aunt, I won't have to hear the negativity that colors my
   feelings about someone I love."
"If I stop going to family dinners on Sundays, I'll be able to
   choose which family members I want to spend time with
   one-on-one."

Reasons We Decide to Make a Change

Change happens when we become tired enough to stop the behaviors that are unhealthy for us.

You Get Tired Enough

The most common reason people change is that they get tired. You can get tired of feeling a certain way, talking about the same problem, dealing with the behavior of others, or a lack of change. There's the saying "I'm sick and tired of being sick and tired." Essentially, you change when you get tired enough of your circumstances.

You Have Finally, Once and for All, Learned the Hard Way

As they say, "Experience is the best teacher." Once you come to terms with the fact that you'll only get more of what you've already received, change becomes the only way out—not changing the other person, but changing your decision to allow your own pain. So you opt out of the cycle.

Not Changing Is Affecting Your Quality of Life

Choosing yourself becomes the only option for having the life you want. At some point, staying the same clearly means choosing dysfunction.

A Significant Life Event Prompts You to Change

Sometimes, becoming a parent and not wanting to inflict the same pain on your child causes you to change. A part of breaking generational cycles is protecting your children from the people who hurt you and haven't changed. Safeguarding your children from the same source of injury allows them to break a cycle. Also, committing to a romantic relationship with someone can change your view about your family relationships. To protect sacred spaces, you may feel compelled to shift family relationships when they're bleeding into your marriage, friendships, relationship with your children, work, and so on.

Common Thoughts That Keep People in Dysfunctional Systems

"I can't set boundaries with my family."

"Blood is thicker than water."

"Your family consists of the only people who will be there for you no matter what."

"There is no one who loves you more than your family."

"That's your ____ [insert unhealthy family member]; you have to have a relationship with them."

"What happens in this house stays in this house."

"You only get one ____ [insert unhealthy family member]; no matter what they did, you need to get over it."

All of these statements are meant to induce guilt and shame, thereby keeping you connected to unhealthy relationships and damaging beliefs. Those statements don't consider how familial relationships cause mental health issues and stunt your ability to thrive. Anyone telling you to accept mistreatment because "it's family" isn't considering your needs. They're considering the more significant needs of the system or trying to maintain the appearance of being problem-free.

In most families, even healthy ones, there are problems. The difference between healthy and unhealthy family dynamics is how problems are handled. If they're covered up, ignored, silenced, or shut down, the system is unhealthy. If the problem is addressed, people are held accountable, and issues are resolved, the system is healthy.

There's no such thing as a problem-free relationship, but some relationships are *highly* problematic. As humans, we have differences and challenges, but those challenges don't have to include abuse, neglect, and the continuation of harm.

EXERCISE

Grab your journal or a piece of paper to complete the following prompts:

❋ How have you defended or upheld unhealthy behaviors in your family?

❋ Using the Stages of Change diagram (see page 78), where are you with your family relationships?

❋ What was the reason you decided to change a relationship with a family member?

CHAPTER 7

Thriving vs. Surviving

"My attention span is short," Whitney told me. At thirty-two years old, she wanted to change her patterns. Whenever she started dating someone, the romance moved fast. She would often move in with a new girlfriend within three months of dating, but by the end of the first year, she would be bored with the relationship and already seeing other people. In her heart, she wanted to find "the one," but through her actions, she was clearly avoiding long-term commitment.

Without fail, after six months of dating, her partners would start to get serious about planning further, while Whitney slowly eased her way out of the relationship. Yet, she wouldn't be direct with her partners about her intentions. This made for explosive and dramatic endings.

While Whitney was growing up, her parents fought loudly and often. When she was sixteen years old, they finally divorced, and to this day, they hate each other. Their on-again, off-again pattern didn't show Whitney how to sustain a healthy partnership. Even though she hated the chaos in her parents' relationship, she was now creating her own version of chaos.

Then Whitney met Sabrina, who called her out on her BS and challenged her in ways that her previous girlfriends hadn't. Sabrina insisted on taking things slow. But as Whitney noticed new parts of herself emerging in the relationship, she felt scared and vulnerable. Still, she wanted to make the relationship work.

She knew she had to rely on role models other than her parents. Her mother often suggested that Whitney was "like her father," a reference that Whitney hated. But in some ways, it was true. She knew she had to learn some new skills because the old ones of lying, cheating, and being passive-aggressive weren't effective.

Whitney decided to start therapy because she knew she needed support to stick to the changes she was making. For years, she had blamed her relationship issues on her partners, but in therapy, she began to acknowledge how she contributed to some of the problems. She came to understand that she was mimicking unhealthy dynamics, so she worked on unlearning dysfunctional patterns and learning how to be in a healthy romantic relationship. Things can be different from what you've always done, and what you've always experienced, in your family.

Thriving vs. Surviving

As a plant mom, I notice when my plants are thriving (flourishing, abundant, and exceeding expectations) and when they're just surviving (languishing, getting by, and existing). When people grow up in dysfunction, they might succumb to the dysfunction, they might survive, or they might thrive. In the previous chapter, I discussed how and why people succumb to dysfunction and the challenges associated with changing. We often say that people "survive" a dysfunctional family, but we rarely acknowledge that people can thrive despite a dysfunctional family.

Thriving suggests that, yes, the environment was impactful, but our personality, determination, and essence superseded our conditions. We can never say who we would have been if we'd grown up in a different environment. But some people have powerfully defied the odds created by their circumstances.

You survive when you don't repeat the cycle, but you thrive when you create a new legacy and trajectory. Conscious awareness and effort are

You thrive when you create a new legacy and trajectory.

what separate someone who thrives from someone who survives. You can consciously create a different life, and those who do are known as "cyclebreakers."

Cyclebreakers

A cyclebreaker is a person who intentionally breaks the pattern of family dysfunction. When you're the first, you often receive more pushback from other family members because you're challenging the family norms.

It isn't easy being the first, because you have to teach yourself a lot of what you need to know to succeed. You learn how to be a different person, with few guides and sometimes no family support. Cyclebreakers are willing to unlearn what wasn't helpful and eager to step outside the box to create a life that works best for them.

Things That Might Be Challenging for Cyclebreakers
- Consistently making decisions in their best interest
- Managing survivor's guilt or remorse
- Dealing with imposter syndrome
- Establishing a healthy support system
- Being transparent about their story because of the fear of judgment
- Finding a community among people with similar experiences

- Remembering to take care of themselves
- Learning to be among people who come from traditional backgrounds
- Learning to adapt to environments with which they have no experience
- Setting limitations on how often and in what ways they can help others

Sometimes, deciding to change yourself means you must distance yourself from people who haven't changed or who uphold unhealthy behaviors. It can be challenging to leave loved ones behind when they don't change along with you. It may make you an outsider in your family.

The changes you make in your personal life can also affect the way the people in your life see themselves. Cyclebreakers care about their family relationships, and they know that some of the relationships will change as the cyclebreaker begins to thrive. If you're the cyclebreaker in your family, others may find it hard to accept the changes because they knew you before you knew yourself. They may have a hard time letting go of who they think you are. You are becoming more of yourself, and that can be hard for people who want to see you only one way—the way that works for them.

In Dysfunctional Families, Change Is Taken Personally

Change can be seen as rejection, even when it's for the better. It can threaten a fractured system because the insinuation is that since you're making changes, everyone else needs to change, too. It's true, however, that when you change yourself, the systems around you will probably indeed change, or at least how you view those systems will change.

When someone rejects you because of how you've changed, the language might sound like this:

"You think you're better than us."
"That isn't how you grew up; why is it like that now?"
"It used to be good enough for you."
"You're acting funny."

Even though others might take your changes personally, you don't have to take their rejection personally. Remember that change is hard, and when someone is resistant to changing, they may criticize you for doing so.

It takes a lot of courage to be open and honest about family struggles. Unfortunately, you can't force anyone else to be courageous.

Being a Victim Might Feel Better Than Accepting Control

It's possible to be victimized without becoming a victim. People can do things to you, but your life doesn't have to become a reflection of what they did. Victims tend to believe they're powerless, even in situations where they own absolute power. I once heard someone at forty years old say, "I'm never going to college, because my parents never talked to me about college." She wasn't in control of her ability to take charge of her life. Even at forty, she still held her parents responsible for what she could currently create for herself.

You aren't a victim of your circumstances. You are who you choose to become in spite of or as a result of your circumstances. Trauma may be a part of your story, but it doesn't reflect the entire person that you are. Even though dysfunction impacts your confidence and desire to try, you can gain confidence through striving.

Victim statements might sound like:

"My parents never taught me ____; therefore, I can't ____."

"It isn't my fault that I never learned how to ____."

"My parents made me this way, so I can't do anything about it."

"I'm not responsible for how I turned out."

How to Disrupt the Pattern of Being a Victim

- Don't make excuses for things that you can control.
- Decide to move forward despite what happened.
- Let go of grudges.
- Acknowledge that you aren't perfect.
- Explore what you've learned.
- Practice assertiveness.
- Stop comparing yourself with others.
- Identify ways that you can better care for yourself.
- Understand your feelings, and learn to express them.
- Minimize or eliminate self-pity (it will keep you stuck).
- Identify what you can control (own your power).

An excellent way to move beyond the identity of victim and take responsibility for your own life is to consider what you've learned from your experiences. For instance:

As a result of the fact that my parents were workaholics:

I developed close relationships with elders outside my family who are still surrogate parents.

I learned how to get to the point quickly because my parents were impatient when I provided many details.

*For Whitney, from the beginning of this chapter, taking responsibil-
  ity might sound like this:*

  My parents didn't teach me what I needed to know about
  healthy relationships. I will learn more by reading, engaging
  with peers who maintain healthy relationships, and going to
  therapy.

Teaching yourself what you were never taught is one of the most powerful ways to become a cyclebreaker.

Be Your Own Best Teacher

First, look within to understand what isn't working in your family's dynamics. Trust that you know when something doesn't feel right and when
it isn't working for you. There's no need to wait for validation from others.

The most important question you need to answer is *What do you want
for your life?* Bear in mind that what you want might not currently exist in
your family.

You might be the first person in your family to

  Make healthy relationship choices
  Make your own decisions
  Set boundaries
  Hold people accountable
  Not attend college
  Attend college
  Practice a different religion
  Not practice a religion
  Challenge the status quo

Not get married

Get married

Be openly LGBTQIA+

Go to therapy

Address your trauma

Preventing Dysfunction When You See Similar Characteristics in Yourself

When you grow up in a dysfunctional family, it can be hard to know what is and isn't dysfunctional. Don't blame yourself for not knowing better. Instead, strive to become more aware.

Awareness allows you to see what you need to change. You might find yourself emulating the behaviors of people you don't want to emulate, which can lead you to change because it's easy to see exactly what you want to work on. But awareness alone will not change you; only action will do that.

Changing who you are as a result of your environment looks like:

Acknowledging the things you want to change

You may find it helpful to make a list of patterns or issues in your family that you'd like to change within yourself. After looking at the list, contemplate how the issues currently affect you and how you exhibit some of the same behaviors you don't like in others.

Owning your issues and not blaming yourself

In the past, you didn't know what you didn't know. Now that you're becoming aware, take ownership of the opportunity to change. Indeed, your family impacted you, but if you aren't making changes, you're choosing to perpetuate the status quo. You're refusing to change what you can. It's no longer them; it's you.

Making small steps toward doing better

It won't be healthy to make a complete life renovation all at once. But in small ways, you can start changing what you say, how you think, and what you do.

If your childhood was unhealthy, as an adult, you can

- Create a family of loving and supportive people (friends, neighbors, elders)
- Set boundaries around how you will allow people to show up in your life
- Choose which relationships from your family of origin are worth maintaining
- Find role models outside your family, and learn from them
- Establish new holiday traditions
- Take and use the parts of your childhood that were healthy, and discard the rest
- Find community among people who are also healing (you are not alone)

Be a Whistleblower in the Family

Issues are usually uncovered by one brave person who is willing to shake things up. Be the brave one in your family. Your level of exposure to the rest of the world may be different from that of other family members. There-fore, you might be more aware of healthier ways to parent, ways to manage emotions without self-medicating, or how to manage finances. Without telling people that they need to change, you can show them or let them know what behaviors no longer work for you.

Small changes in a dysfunctional family might look like:

- Liz never heard her mother say "I love you." As an adult, Liz initi-ates telling her mother, "I love you," and after several months, her mother starts saying, "I love you, too."
- As a child, Brent was often spanked for even minor infractions. He chooses not to spank his own children. When family members have opposed his "new age" parenting practices, he tells them he's doing things differently.
- Kim's father introduced her to alcohol when she was just twelve years old. He thought it was OK for her to have an occasional beer. When Kim turned twenty-three, she stopped drinking with her father.

Family isn't your only teacher; you have many. Be willing to look be-yond your family for healthy ways of being. If you didn't learn something at home, there are so many other places to learn it. "No one taught me" isn't a reason to give up.

You learn a lot from your family, and you can also learn from

Reading books, newspapers, or magazines
Listening to podcasts
Watching TV
Observing how other families interact with each other
Learning about other cultures

Travel

Therapy (individual, couples, and/or group)

Social media

If you have a complex family relationship, it's normal to

***Feel envious of people who had more ideal family relation-
ships.*** Watching someone experience the life you wanted can
be painful. It's important to remember that you didn't pick
your family, nor did the person you envy pick theirs. Be mindful
of your energy when you notice jealousy. Be kind to yourself,
but don't allow your envy to take control of you emotionally.

***Wonder if you'd be different if your experiences had been dif-
ferent.*** Playing the game of "what if" is dangerous because it
ropes you into a fantasy that you'll never be able to control.

***Not talk about your family because you fear people won't un-
derstand.*** There will be people who have no clue about your
experiences, yet they'll offer feedback about how you should
engage with your family. The simple advice is to ignore them,
but we know how hard that can be. So respond to them instead of ignoring them. Send the message that their feedback
isn't welcome.

Responding to people who disagree with your beliefs about
family might sound like:

"My family seems different from yours. I understand your
perspective, and I hope you understand mine."

"All families are different."

"Please don't tell me how to be in a relationship with my family."

"This is the way I choose to handle my issues with my family."

Ignore big problems in the relationship to get along. To keep the peace, you might find yourself ignoring significant issues in your relationships. But you aren't keeping the peace if only the other person is at peace while you are not. Over time, problems that are ignored become bigger.

Pretend things are better than they are. Appearances are important to many families. In an attempt to appear "normal," you may behave out of obligation or to keep up a social standard rather than act based on the truth. Pretending is a coping strategy used to reduce guilt and shame. Convincing yourself, *If everything looks OK, then it must be OK*. You may post photos and stories online that depict a perfect relationship with your mother when the opposite is true.

Try to be the opposite of your family. Becoming the exact opposite of your family isn't always best, because in many dysfunctional systems, there are a few things that work well. Julie told me, "My mother was a workaholic, but she never missed bedtime with my siblings and me." People can be more than one thing and, therefore, not all bad. Perhaps there are a few healthy things in your family that you don't mind repeating.

Struggle to have a healthy relationship with your family. As
an adult, you might find it hard to figure out how to coexist
with certain family members who caused you harm as a child
or in adulthood. There's no true definition of a "normal" family, as you define what feels suitable for you in your relationships. Infrequent contact can be normal, or speaking to a
family member daily can be normal.

EXERCISE

Grab your journal or a piece of paper to complete the following prompts:

* What habits do you possess that are similar to those of your
  family of origin?
* What small changes have you attempted to make in your
  family?
* What is your definition of a "normal" family?

CHAPTER 8

How to Manage Relationships with People Who Won't Change

When Tiffany was a child, her mother, Rita, always seemed to be in financial trouble. They were evicted, and their utilities were disconnected too many times, causing them to move in with various family members. Rita's mother often took them in and helped out, but she died ten years ago.

Then it fell to Tiffany to take care of her mother. For seven years, they had been on a roller-coaster ride. Rita would briefly move into her own place, but she'd end up back at Tiffany's within a few months because she simply couldn't pay her bills. Rita had a full-time job, but she was a poor money manager. As a result, Tiffany believed she'd always have to take care of her mom financially. But she resented it because she was already a single mom with two boys to support.

Even when she was in college and working part-time, Tiffany sometimes sent Rita money to prevent her from being evicted. As a result of her upbringing, Tiffany made sure she was the opposite of her mother. She pinched pennies, carefully combed over her finances, paid bills on time, and had a savings account. Bravely and without direction, she decided to be more fiscally responsible because she wanted to create a different outcome for herself and her children.

But Tiffany felt it was her obligation to help her mother. At least Rita stuck around and was a fairly decent parent, while Tiffany's father was never present physically—and barely financially. Tiffany struggled to accept her mother and frequently lectured her about poor money habits. But Rita couldn't seem to meet her daughter's expectations.

Tiffany knew her mom had always been fiscally irresponsible, but she thought it was because Rita didn't want to listen and follow her wise guidance. Tiffany didn't realize her mother was dealing with her own internal barriers. Tiffany just hoped that she could learn to support her mother without feeling so resentful all the time.

It's important to recognize that two things can be true at the same time. You can love your family and also have deep wounds due to those relationships. Tiffany needed to embrace the duality of feeling hurt by her mother while also loving her mother.

Parents Are People with Children

Remember that parents were people before they had children. Parenting doesn't necessarily make us more responsible, wise, forgiving, or less angry—or anything else. Being a parent literally means nothing more than being a human with a child.

Growth involves seeing your parents as people outside of their roles as your parents. Before Rita was Tiffany's mom, she was Rita without a child. Perhaps her spending was less damaging when she was an individual without the obligation to take care of anyone else. It's possible that the cost of parenting didn't align with Rita's lifestyle choices. Yes, she was responsible for her child, but she couldn't provide for herself and another human being.

It makes sense that we expect our parents to rise above who they are in order to care for us, but they are who they are until they take steps to change. For Rita, change is possible, but she must be willing to do it. We humans are complex, and changing who we are can be a difficult process.

You Can't Change People—So Don't Hold Your Breath Waiting for Them to Change

Acceptance isn't easy, but it makes life more peaceful. When the solution to the problem is "they need to change," the problem will never go away. You can only control your side of the street. You can't make people mow their lawn, pick up their trash, or do anything else on their side of the street. You only have the authority to do your part *You can only* in the relationship to coexist with people who *control your side* won't or can't change. If you don't want to leave, *of the street.* you need tools to accept the situation as it is.

People are not Legos. You can't decide what you want them to look like. Acceptance means allowing them to be who they are, whether you agree with it or not. This doesn't mean you're giving up. It just means you give in to what already exists and claim your peace. Fighting against acceptance creates continual chaos in relationships. Acceptance doesn't mean you have to tolerate behavior that impacts you. Instead, you choose how you want to manage what you can't change about others.

When I was in the seventh grade in Detroit public schools, my teacher announced at the beginning of the school year that she wouldn't break up any fights in her class. My initial thought was, "Everybody's going to fight in this class." But the opposite occurred. I remember just one disturbance in her class the whole year.

Kids may want to fight, but they expect adults to break it up. When my teacher permitted us to fight, we thought about whether it was the appropriate environment for chaos without intervention. By accepting that kids would inevitably try to fight in middle school, she allowed us to decide to be better through our own doing. Allow people to change without telling them what they need to change.

Setting Boundaries When You Can't Change People

You can only change your reaction when people are inevitably themselves. For my teacher, it was, "I will not be physically harmed by getting in the way."

For Tiffany, healthy boundaries might look like:

- Allowing her mother to stay if she contributes by helping with the grandchildren
- Setting aside a budgeted monthly amount to offer her
- Inviting her mother to stay long-term to end the back-and-forth
- Going to therapy to process her resentment

For Tiffany, healthy boundaries are not:

- Forcing her mother to save money
- Lecturing her when she overspends
- Shaming her into changing her behaviors

Shaming People Doesn't Make Them Better

Instead of changing them in a positive way, research has found that shaming kids makes them more aggressive. Whether children or adults, shaming people lowers their self-esteem, leading them to engage in more of the behaviors you don't want. In fact, many studies have indicated that fat shaming causes people to gain weight. So shaming isn't an effective tool for anything, yet people still use it to try to get others to change.

In the movie *Full Metal Jacket*, a soldier in training is body-shamed and ridiculed by sergeants and comrades for his perceived lack of intelligence. The shaming leads him to mental collapse, homicide, and eventually death by suicide. That's certainly not the intended behavior of someone you want to turn into a better soldier.

Again, shaming isn't a change agent. It's a way to make people feel terrible for simply being who they are. We have to face the reality that sometimes people can change and sometimes they can't. As an outsider, it's hard to determine who can and can't change, what barriers they might be facing, and the obstacles their internal dialogue may be creating for them. Pushing others to be different deflects from changing what we *can* control.

Do Your Part

In many cases, people stay in unhealthy relationships and continue to struggle because they don't have the tools to make their relationship healthier. They believe the only way for anything to get better is for the *other* person to change.

You can amend your beliefs about the abilities of others, reorder your expectations, and tackle tough conversations that can potentially change your relationships. But you can't in any way change people, no matter how hard you try. When you see a person change because of someone else, it usually doesn't last, because they're just pretending and can't keep that up for very long. It's hard to pretend to want something that others want for you. Every person walking the planet, even your mother, father, sister, brother, and so on, has the right to live in whatever way they want. You have to want to change for yourself. This isn't an easy thing to accept, but it's necessary to stop us from fighting with others because they aren't who we want them to be.

Things You Can Change When People Don't Change
Your Beliefs About Others' Abilities
One of my favorite personal finance books, *You Only Live Once* by Jason Vitug, talks about money management principles with a heavy focus on mindset. Tiffany is trying to change her mother's mindset, but Rita isn't interested even though she suffers the consequences of her spending habits. She's just not ready to change.

Perhaps it would be helpful for Tiffany to consider this:

- Money management isn't easy, which is why there are so many books on the topic.
- Old habits are familiar.
- Doing something different isn't as easy as it seems.

Your Expectations
Expectations are healthy but should be based on the individual, not their role in your life. Parenthood doesn't automatically mean that a person will know how to handle finances. Becoming a parent doesn't equip you with money management skills.

Perhaps it would be helpful for Tiffany to consider this:

- "My mother struggles to manage her finances."
- "My mother is unwilling to change her outlook."
- "My mother is good at many things, but managing money isn't one of them."

Your Conversations and Statements
Stop pretending that things are normal, and give up staying silent to keep the peace. Healthy relationships require tough conversations and boundaries.

Perhaps it would be helpful for Tiffany to consider

- How she wants to help her mother and how to phrase her statements:

    "I'm willing to allow you to stay with me indefinitely."

    "I will allow you to stay with me for one year, and after that time, I'd like you to be in a position to move out."

- How to communicate her expectations:

    "While you're living here, I want you to pay the electric bill."

    "It might be helpful for both of us to maintain a household budget."

- What to say to her mother when financial boundaries are crossed:

    "You agreed to pay the electric bill, and it's overdue. Please give me the money by Friday."

    "We agreed that you would help with childcare on Tuesdays. Please be available next time."

Helping vs. Enabling

When you're helping others, it's essential to be aware of the difference between helping and enabling. Honestly, helping others will not be detrimental to you, but enabling them will.

These behaviors are enabling and not helpful:

- Excusing the negative choices of others
- Ignoring that someone has a problem
- Doing things for people that they can do for themselves
- Finding solutions for people instead of allowing them to find answers on their own

- Offering money and resources when you can't do so comfortably
- Preventing people from enduring the consequences of their actions
- Not setting boundaries around how to help others

Distance Is a Coping Strategy

When you're ambivalent about staying in a relationship and not ready to leave, it's OK to create some distance between yourself and the other person. Distancing yourself is strategic and can start with the small step of making yourself less available to them.

In dysfunctional families, a conversation about your need for space can end in one of two ways: your request is honored or the relationship is damaged. You know which family members can handle a discussion about your need for space and which ones might do better if you take space without a direct explanation, based on how they've responded in the past.

Some of the reasons you may find yourself needing to take a break:

- Your energy is adversely affected by interactions with the person.
- You become easily frustrated or short-tempered when you're with them.
- You feel that your boundaries aren't honored.
- You don't feel comfortable being yourself around this person.
- You're in a different season of your life.

As our priorities and interests shift, our people may shift as well. If you've developed an interest in plants, for example, you might want to be around other people with the same interest. Likewise, if all your friends are going through a divorce while you're trying to make your marriage work, you may not want to be around them. It's OK to focus on your needs and take a pause.

Recognize, however, that ignoring people isn't the same as distancing yourself. Both might achieve the same goal of creating space, but ignoring someone is passive and lacks intention. Distancing is an intentional process to allow you to maintain the relationship.

Distancing can look like:

- Allowing a person's call to go to voicemail and calling them back when you're in the right headspace to talk
- Steering the conversation away from topics you aren't comfortable discussing
- Directly declining an invitation
- Not asking people to be involved in certain aspects of your life

Ignoring can look like:

- Not following up with people
- Shutting people out completely
- Being indirect when someone requests something of you

With distance, you can stay in a relationship while taking the space you need, as long as the other person respects your boundaries. Of course, distance may not be an option in abusive relationships where the other person does *not* respect your boundaries. Engaging with people less often can be a method for preserving a relationship.

Shifting Your Role

If you're known for being a certain way, that doesn't mean you have to stay the same. You can shift your role in your family to fit who you are today. If you were once the responsible one, it doesn't mean you always have to be the responsible one. Once the quiet one, not always the quiet one. Who are you really beyond the labels you've been assigned? Start being yourself in your family as a way of shifting your role within it.

At first, your other family members will be surprised to see the changes in you. Allow them to be shocked without going back to the version of yourself that doesn't fit what you're now trying to create in your family.

Acceptance Gives You Peace

The discussion of acceptance bears repeating: stop letting others get under your skin when they're simply being themselves. When people don't change, you can change your reaction to them. Tiffany decided to no longer be shocked by her mother's spending habits, and in so doing, she found peace. This doesn't mean, of course, that she ignores or allows her mother's behavior to be harmful to her.

When people don't change, you can change your reaction to them.

If you aren't sure how to respond, think about how you've handled unwanted behaviors in the past, and try something different. Determine how you would ideally respond in the future, and start making small steps toward responding in a way that feels good for you instead of reverting to familiar unhealthy patterns.

It's OK to be bothered, and you don't have to pretend that you aren't. Nevertheless, acceptance and shifting your role can help you feel less bothered.

If you want to maintain relationships with people who won't change, it's up to you to make changes. You will have to do the work to accept situations and build patience for what is outside your control. Remember that dealing with certain problematic behaviors is a choice. If you choose to maintain the relationship because it's worth keeping, you're making a choice to stay even if it means struggling to accept the other person.

You can't pick your family, but you can decide who you want to have in your life. All adult relationships are a choice. No one is forc-

All adult relationships are a choice.

ing you to be in an unhealthy relationship. You will be presented with the same problems until you commit to making different choices.

Say This to Yourself: "I am choosing to stay in this relationship despite what the relationship is. I am not stuck, I am not powerless, and I am making a choice."

EXERCISE

Grab your journal or a piece of paper to complete the following prompts:

* What have you attempted to change about a family member?
* What do you need to change about handling certain problematic behaviors?
* What are you able to control in the relationship?

CHAPTER 9

Ending Relationships When Others Won't Change

Jacob's parents were never married to each other, and his father, Bruce, had been in and out of his life. Bruce seemed to have symptoms of post-traumatic stress disorder and bouts of depression, but he was never formally diagnosed. He was often agitated, paranoid, withdrawn, or verbally aggressive, which made it difficult for him to get along with others. Everyone (except Bruce) knew and accepted that he was struggling with mental health issues. It was the norm for him to steal the show at family events by arguing and causing a scene.

As a result, Jacob was tired of the constant chaos and ready to end his relationship with his father. He had tried several strategies, from changing himself, to accepting the situation, to ignoring Bruce's offensive behaviors. Yet, his dad's actions only seemed to get worse, as he did more and more things that Jacob needed to somehow forgive and accept.

For a few weeks, Jacob tried to convince his dad to try therapy, but Bruce became defensive about it, always blaming his issues on others. Sometimes, he blamed his problems on his upbringing, and other times, he accused people of mistreating him. Whenever Jacob tried to talk about important topics, Bruce would shut down and disappear for weeks or months.

Jacob considered how ending the relationship with his dad would affect others in the family, but he was done and wanted peace. He just wanted the break to cause as few casualties as possible.

The Impact of Mental Health Issues on Relationships

Everyone has mental health ups and downs, but some people have serious issues that affect their ability to maintain healthy relationships. In his book *Depression Is Contagious*, Michael Yapko discusses how parental mental health can affect children. Attachment is damaged, for example, when mothers are depressed. They may speak less often to their children, be unsupportive, or seem emotionally unavailable.

Most of the statistics we have about mental health care are based on formally diagnosed people, yet there are large numbers of people with undiagnosed disorders that are severe enough to harm their relationships. In many dysfunctional relationships, mental health issues are untreated and ignored, but a problem can't be repaired if we pretend it doesn't exist. Of course, diagnosis doesn't guarantee someone will manage their relationships any better.

Nevertheless, some dysfunctional families enable those with mental health problems rather than help them. While growing up, I was taught that some people had mental health issues that needed tending but that those issues were to be accepted. "That's just how they are," I was told. Sometimes, however, "how they were" was abusive, dismissive, mean, and sabotaging. What if we were to stop making excuses and collectively encourage these family members to get the mental health support they need?

This can be challenging since therapy is still considered taboo in many families. The whole family is affected when one person decides to go to therapy because individual changes impact the whole family system. Conversely, when therapy isn't sought, families continue to grapple with the same issues over and over. Depression, anxiety, mood, personality issues, and other mental health issues are often the main causes of relationship fractures.

Depression

Depression presents at differing levels of severity. Some people can move through life despite their depression, while others are consumed by it and unable to engage in the world.

In relationships, depression can look like:

- Crying often, with no known cause
- Losing interest in things that were once enjoyable
- Ghosting (disappearing abruptly from people and obligations)
- Feeling withdrawn around people
- Being easily irritated
- Constantly feeling angry
- Having frequent melancholia
- Neglecting duties
- Being emotionally unavailable

Anxiety

Social phobias, PTSD, and general anxiety can also have detrimental effects on relationships. Anxiety involves racing thoughts, worry, and/or preoccupation with the past or future. It can even cause physical discomfort, such as diarrhea and skin rashes. Most people experience anxiety to some extent, but fewer people find that it inhibits their life in a significant way.

In relationships, anxiety can look like:

- Not participating in a social gathering
- Showing up inconsistently
- Being in chronic emotional distress
- Intrusively violating boundaries
- Making promises and underdelivering
- Sabotaging yourself or someone else
- Feeling paranoid about someone's words or actions

Personality Issues

Borderline, narcissistic, and dependent personality disorders tend to cause the most relationship issues. Unlike depression or anxiety, a personality disorder can be more pervasive. People with specific personality symptoms may find it challenging to maintain relationships, not just with those in their family, but also with friends, romantic partners, and business colleagues.

In relationships, personality issues can look like:

- Blaming others
- Showing high reactivity
- Reinventing the truth
- Chronic gaslighting
- Being unable to respect and implement boundaries
- Having difficulty making healthy decisions
- Behaving erratically
- Being self-absorbed

Without a formal diagnosis, labeling a mental health issue isn't always helpful, however. Instead, focus on the behaviors you see and how they get in the way of your relationship with the other person. Nevertheless, you can't control how someone manages their mental health. Often, people go to therapy but still don't change as you expect or within the time frame you'd prefer. All you can do in that situation is take care of your own mental health.

Unlearning That Mistreatment Is Acceptable If It's Family

When people say, "You have to love your family no matter what," they may not understand or comprehend the "what" that has caused you to create distance or end a relationship. Being family doesn't give anyone a get-out-of-jail-free pass. Even in family relationships, there can be consequences for harming others.

Perhaps the only way to love certain family members and be well is to love them from a distance. In doing this, you're choosing self-preservation and self-love. It isn't an uncomplicated choice, but it might be the healthiest one for you. Remember that "love" is a verb, and action is needed to sustain relationships. When there aren't any beneficial actions to support the relationship, you lose the ability to maintain it. So when staying is harder, leaving becomes an option.

As a therapist, I have seen people develop their own depression, anxiety, and severe mental health issues as a result of trying to maintain unhealthy relationships with family members. We aren't naturally inclined to drop these relationships or change how we show up in them, so we hold on, hoping that something will change. If you've arrived at the place of wanting to sever a relationship, you've likely already tried everything you can to stay.

Remember This: You don't have to accept mistreatment from people just because you're related to them. You don't have to stay in unhealthy relationships because of shared history. Healthy relationships are rooted in love, mutual respect, and connection. Ask yourself: Is this relationship supportive of my values and what I want in my life?

Estrangement

Severing ties with one or more family members is called estrangement, and it's more common than we may care to acknowledge. Sometimes, the estrangement is intended to be short-term, used as a pause, or it may be long-term with no plans to reconcile.

Two types of estrangement can occur: intentional emotional detachment or physical estrangement with termination of all contact.

Estrangement may sometimes seem sudden, but the cutoff often happens when the person who leaves has had enough. So it doesn't really happen out of the blue, as seeds of judgment, differing beliefs, mistrust, chaos, and/or trauma have been present, often for many years.

Family rifts can feel shameful or embarrassing to some as they struggle to control the narrative or image of the family. Dr. Karl Pillemer, author of *Fault Lines: Fractured Families and How to Mend Them*, has identified six top reasons for estrangement:

1. Issues in the relationship since childhood
2. Divorce that created resentment, animosity, and the choosing of sides
3. Fights over money, including loans and inheritances
4. Unmet needs and a repeated failure to adhere to boundaries
5. Differences in beliefs, lifestyles, and values
6. Ongoing challenges with in-laws

The leading cause of estrangement for mothers and daughters, for example, is a difference in values. Mothers who are divorced are more likely to have estranged relationships with their children, likely due to the negative impact of the father and mother's relationship.

Dealing with Guilt After Estrangement

When I worked with children in the foster care system, even in the worst circumstances, children wanted to be with their families. They wanted to forgive and move forward even when it wasn't healthy, because "it's family." We often feel a deep sense of connection and loyalty toward family despite mistreatment. So when someone decides to sever ties, they know it's likely others won't accept it.

Guilt is one of the primary emotions we experience in this situation. This is natural since we live in a society that supports the narrative of "blood is thicker than water." Few exceptions are made for those of us who endure trauma, abuse, and dysfunction at the hands of family members. Others might assume the person ending the relationship is cold, when in fact that person is wounded and feels justified, though often conflicted, in their decision.

Moments That Might Prompt Feelings of Guilt After Estrangement
Holidays
Birthdays
Dreams
Seeing old family photos
Anniversaries of deaths and family events
Seeing someone with an ideal family relationship

Everyone sees circumstances from their own perspective. People who have healthy relationships with their family may find it hard to understand why someone else might choose to sever ties. But no one else can determine how much anyone can or should endure.

A Few Reminders for People with Difficult Family Relationships

- You are not alone. There's no such thing as a "perfect" family.
- You aren't obligated to have relationships with unhealthy people.
- You don't have to like every person in your family.
- You can't create healthy relationships with people who aren't interested in having healthy relationships.
- When you speak your truth, you aren't betraying anyone; you're honoring yourself.
- It's OK to be different from the other people in your family.
- You can create family relationships with people who aren't related to you.

> *You aren't obligated to have relationships with unhealthy people.*

After years of physical and emotional abuse, Jamie ended her relationship with her mother. From friends, she often heard, "You only get one mother." That statement and others like it sent her into a spiral of guilt. She repeatedly questioned if she was doing the right thing. Yet, without her mom in her life, she felt more at ease, and her days were less chaotic.

It might be helpful for Jamie to say this:

- "I understand that your relationship with your mother might be different from mine. Please don't tell me what's best for me."
- "After much consideration, I decided to end my relationship with my mother because it was the healthiest option for me."
- "I wish the situation were different, but it isn't. It doesn't help when you tell me what I should do."

It's perfectly fine to let other people know it isn't OK for them to tell you what to do in your relationships with other people, especially those who have harmed you. When someone chooses to end a relationship with a family member, it's almost never based on one thing, and it isn't an easy decision. Often, the relationship has ended after many rounds of forgiveness and trying to make it work. When we encounter someone who has decided to let go of a relationship that disturbed their peace and caused them mental or emotional stress, we should offer them grace instead of opinions.

Consider saying this when people ask about your relationship with an estranged family member:

- "After many rounds of trying to work through things, I no longer have a relationship with my father."
- "I'm unsure how she's doing because we don't talk anymore."
- "This is a touchy subject for me because we don't have a relationship anymore."

You may also choose not to be direct on this subject. When asked, "How's your mom?" Charlotte found it easier to say, "She's well," instead of telling the other person that she no longer talks to her mother. When you're direct about the relationship, your transparency may spark other questions, such as "What happened? Do you think you'll reconnect?" Or the person may share their opinion: "I would never stop talking to my mother." Estrangement is usually not an easy choice; instead, it is necessary. You can share whichever version of the truth you feel most comfortable handling.

Self-Induced Guilt

Relationships with family can be complicated, especially when the assumption is that you'll provide perpetual forgiveness. It's OK if you're tired of forgiving the same person for the same thing, even when they're family.

You can decide if you want to forgive and move forward or forgive and release. But forgiving and forgetting won't change difficult situations.

You might feel guilty when you make a choice that's healthy for you but disappointing to others. But guilt isn't necessarily an indication that you're doing something wrong.

Survivor's Guilt

Feeling bad for getting out of an unhealthy situation and leaving others behind is a form of survivor's guilt. It's unlikely that we can help people more than they want to be helped. It's hard to watch people suffer when we know what will help them, but we can't force them to do what we see as best for them, as that violates their free will.

We cause ourselves suffering when we try to do more than we can for others. Older siblings sometimes experience guilt for leaving their siblings in chaotic home environments, for example. It can be painful to move on when we know those we love have to remain in the turmoil. But staying in chaos to be present for others isn't healthy. In the long run, leaving will likely put you in a better position to help your siblings if they truly want the help.

In the memoir *The Glass Castle*, author Jeannette Walls describes leaving home before completing high school, and most of her younger siblings later followed suit. Only their youngest sister chose to stay with their parents into young adulthood. As the oldest, Jeannette Walls was sad to leave her siblings behind, yet she knew she couldn't stay and save them. Building a life and inviting them into it would be more helpful than living in chaos along with them. And ultimately, she couldn't save her youngest sister because her sister didn't want to be free.

We can let go of guilt by acknowledging that not everyone wants the same things as we do, or that they might not currently have the tools to make a change.

Sometimes, Even Being Around Someone in Small Doses Is Still Too Much

Dana wanted a relationship with her brother, Carlos, so she tried for years. When he stole her identity, she forgave him. When he started false rumors in the family about her, she forgave him. Then, he started pressuring her to communicate with him more often. She couldn't. Giving Carlos more access only gave him more opportunities to take advantage of her. Dana loved her brother, but she was tired of being victimized by him. Distance wasn't working, as it only made him more persistent about gaining access. Then, their father intervened and insisted that Dana talk to Carlos more because "he's your brother."

She felt anxious, angry, and misunderstood, which led to sleep problems, headaches, and concentration difficulties. Dana didn't want to stop talking to her brother, but she knew that was the only way she could find relief. When people repeat the behaviors they apologize for, it voids the apology. At some point, they often use up all their forgiveness credits.

It might be helpful for Dana to say something like this to her father:

- "Stop trying to persuade me to stay in an unhealthy family relationship because you believe family is everything, no matter what. You're advising me to stay in a harmful, abusive, and intensely stressful situation. Encouraging me to push through this is not supportive. Would you please help me do what's best for me, even if you'd personally do something different? I tried everything I could to stay in this relationship, and now I'm ready to release it with love."

How to handle someone choosing to end a relationship or be estranged from you:

- Sometimes, when you want to reconnect, you might attempt to force the other person to speak to you. Respect their boundaries of estrangement or distance.
- Go to therapy to get help with grieving the relationship.
- Make necessary changes in other relationships to ensure they remain healthy.

Toxic Forgiveness

Toxic forgiveness is an unhealthy way that people pretend to be unharmed, over it, or forgetful of the offense. Forgiving to keep the peace or as a way of people-pleasing is not healthy for your mental health or your relationships. Take time to process your pain, slowly rebuild trust, and decide if you need to show up differently in the relationship. Forgiving and forgetting is not a realistic approach to moving forward.

In most cases, we aren't really forgiving and forgetting; we are forgiving and repressing. In families, it can be the norm to move on without processing what happened, what will be different moving forward, and the feelings that arose as a result of what happened. You can't "move on" without working through what's really going on.

Common Myths About Forgiveness
Myth: Once you've forgiven, you can't talk about it anymore
Holding on to emotions without processing them is never healthy, so you may still feel the need to talk about the situation after you decide to forgive someone. Whenever you experience a traumatic event, the memories may continue to haunt you. To move through experiences like these, it can be helpful to talk to a mental health professional or a trusted person who can help you make sense of these feelings in a meaningful way.

Venting to friends and family may not be healthy, however, if you simply talk about the problem over and over with no attempt at resolution. Progress-focused venting involves attempting to understand the complete picture, processing your feelings and thoughts, and determining what could help you feel better and move on.

Myth: Once you've forgiven, you must stay in an unhealthy relationship

Forgiveness doesn't mean reconciliation. Based on the offense or its intensity, you may choose to forgive and move on without maintaining the connection. You can decide what the relationship will look like after forgiveness.

Myth: If you forgive them once, you have to forgive them in the future

Forgiveness doesn't mean you accept the same behavior over and over. People don't get a pass to repeat the offense. You can decide how many times you want to forgive and move forward with someone or when you want to forgive and sever the connection. Forgiveness and what you do afterward are your choices to make.

Myth: When you forgive, you can no longer feel upset or angry

Forgiveness doesn't mean you have to ignore what they did or how their behavior made you feel. A University of Michigan study found that the best way to deal with troubling feelings is to step back and talk about the feelings using third-person language. For instance, "Why did she feel that way when her mother-in-law said that about her weight?" The "she" in the question is you. Detaching yourself from the experience can help you develop objectivity about your emotions and minimize the self-pity that can keep you stuck and unable to move on.

Myth: When you forgive, you have to forget what happened

You can't erase your memories or feelings, and either may come up at uncomfortable moments. "Forgive and forget" is an expression, not something we can achieve in a literal sense. You'll likely forgive and feel less of an impact, but you may never get over the experience entirely.

Forgiving for Your Own Peace of Mind

The hardest people to forgive are those who don't believe they harmed you and don't apologize or ask for forgiveness. Therefore, when you forgive them, you do it for your own sense of closure and to reduce the many negative thoughts you have about them. While forgiveness is certainly not required, it does make some of us feel better. With forgiveness, we gift ourselves peace.

With forgiveness, we gift ourselves peace.

Even though not everyone and everything deserves our forgiveness, it still feels freeing to forgive. Remember that it isn't a pass for what they did or an opportunity for them to have access to you. Forgiveness is simply a release so that they no longer own your energy. It releases the hold they have over you, allowing you to let go of at least a significant amount of resentment, anger, rage, and fear. It isn't an easy or comfortable journey, but it's even more uncomfortable to hold on to those negative emotions.

Ultimately, however, forgiveness is a choice. In an Instagram poll, I asked, "Are some things unforgivable?" Eighty-nine percent of people answered yes, while 11 percent answered no, saying that everything is forgivable. Based on the results, some people are willing to forgive everything, but most people aren't.

Waiting for an Apology

You may never get the apology you deserve from someone who has wronged you, and even if they do apologize, it might not help you feel any better about what happened.

- Some people won't apologize even when the facts are in front of them.
- Some people don't think you deserve an apology.
- Some people blame you ("You made me do it").
- Some people apologize with actions, not words.
- Some people won't apologize because of their ego.
- Some people will break if they admit the truth.
- Some people don't have the tools to be accountable for their actions.

If we want to stay connected to someone who has hurt us, we have to meet them where they are and accept what they're capable of offering.

Forgiving Yourself

The most complicated person to forgive is yourself. We can go into a spiral of self-loathing when we realize we stayed in a relationship too long, allowed too much abuse, or accepted less than we deserved. Then, when we choose to leave, there's the guilt about walking away. If you've left a family relationship, know that you acted in your best interest after trying for perhaps years to make it work. Be compassionate with yourself for making a tough decision when you felt there was no other option.

When You Decide to End a Family Relationship, It Might Affect Other Family Relationships

Dana's father didn't want to feel awkward if his children stopped speaking to each other. So even though Dana was being mistreated by her brother consistently, her dad wanted her to preserve the relationship and maintain appearances.

Deciding to end a relationship with one family member might cause other family members to feel ashamed or embarrassed. It might also highlight the dysfunction in the family and bring secrets and denials to the forefront. Families often maintain unspoken rules that limit our ability to make healthy choices for ourselves.

Most family members want you to be happy and will support your decisions, but when you need to end an unhealthy family relationship, they may not understand that your happiness depends on that decision. In that case, they need to step outside the situation.

What you can say to family members to encourage them to step outside the situation:

- "If I had a relationship with a partner who stole money from me, would you tell me to stay in the relationship?"
- "If a stranger sexually assaulted me, would you encourage me to contact authorities or to maintain a relationship with my abuser?"
- "If my friend was sharing my personal business after I asked them not to, would you suggest I continue the relationship with that friend?"

Common Things You Might Experience When Severing Ties

Gaslighting

Not noticing a problem is the best way to exist within a family's dysfunctional system. When you communicate that something isn't healthy or normal, you might suddenly be seen as the problem while your family ignores the real issue. Families often pretend there are no problems, so talking about issues is perceived as a threat to the system.

For example, abuse is the real problem, but talking about the abuse may *become* the problem to the family. Emotional neglect is a real problem, but any utterance of childhood issues could be seen as the problem.

Gaslighting Statements

"You're not the only person who deals with this. Other people have it worse."

"You made that up."

"Why are you saying things to hurt people?"

"That's the past, and you don't need to bring it up."

"You need to get over it."

"It wasn't that bad."

Denial

It's unhealthy to teach people that family is everything, even when the family is dysfunctional. No one should be convinced to ignore abuse, trauma, or mistreatment. Persuading people to stay in unhealthy relationships for the sake of family harms their mental health, especially if the family frowns on outside relationships. This isolates people from having healthy connections with others. You can have healthy family relationships and healthy relationships outside the family, and the two need not compete.

Every year around the holidays, people tell me they feel anxious, depressed, or angry about "having to" spend the holidays with family. In some cases, these experiences include sharing meals with the person who abused them, enduring verbal abuse during their visit, or watching their siblings' needs be prioritized over their own. Ignoring big problems can hurt. If you disregard the truth to exist in a relationship, there will be consequences mentally and emotionally (and sometimes physically).

Family should be held to a higher standard, not a lower one. The relationships within families are more long-term and impactful, so ideally, they should be the healthiest ones we have.

How to Handle Engaging with People You Choose Not to Have in Your Life

Because it's family, you may sometimes be exposed to people you no longer want in your life. Other family members may ask about the relationship, or you might be physically placed in situations with that person. For instance, if you severed ties with your aunt but want to celebrate your grandmother's birthday, you will likely have to deal with your aunt's attendance at the party.

Here's how you can manage an in-person interaction:

- Say "hello" to the family member if you feel comfortable doing so.
- Maintain social distancing.
- Warn other family members not to force an interaction between the two of you.

It's also your prerogative to decline events where certain people will be present. Depending on the offense, it can be harmful to reexpose yourself to someone who harmed you. Forcing yourself to socially engage with some people can trigger mental and emotional setbacks. Know yourself well enough to understand when you can't be around certain people, and make a commitment to take good care of yourself. For instance, if the thought of seeing a family member increases your anxiety, leads to moodiness, or increases your propensity to engage in negative behaviors, you are being triggered. Be proactive about taking care of yourself when you notice your triggers.

Should You Allow Your Children to Maintain Relationships with People You No Longer See?

Severing ties may impact not only you—doing so could impact your children if they have a relationship with the family member. Part of your responsibility as a parent is determining the people your child should have relationships with. Depending on why you ended the relationship, you may decide to no longer allow your children to see the person either.

Here are a few questions to determine whether to end the relationship for your children or allow it to continue:

- Did the person have a healthy relationship with your children before the disconnection with you?
- Can the person maintain a relationship with your children without talking to them about the issues between you?
- Has your child asked to maintain contact with the person? If so, will it be emotionally and physically safe for them to have contact?
- Can you trust the family member with your child?

What to Say to Family Members Who Question Your Decision or Attempt to Force Communication

- "The relationship isn't healthy for me, so I choose not to engage."
- "I know it's hard for you to understand, but it's my choice, and I need you to respect my choices."
- "Please stop trying to pressure me to speak to someone who harmed me."
- "We don't feel the same way about the situation. Please allow me to have my perspective."
- "You're pushing me to do something that's not good for me."

Unquestioned Loyalty

Questions are a healthy way to understand systems, including families. It isn't OK when you aren't allowed to ask questions or when questions are unanswered. Critical thinking is a threat to unhealthy systems, and questions make people think. So people often fight it when the system is questioned. Still, your loyalty is first and foremost to your own well-being.

EXERCISE

Grab your journal or a piece of paper to complete the following prompts:

* What relationships were affected when you ended a relationship with a family member, or what relationship do you feel might be affected if you sever a relationship?
* What are your thoughts on forgiveness? Is it necessary? Are some things unforgivable? If so, what's unforgivable?

CHAPTER 10

Building Support Outside Your Family

Dan's mother worked, and he saw his father infrequently. His brother and sister were already old enough that they had moved out of the house. While his mom was at work, Dan stayed with his neighbors, the Reddings, and on weekends, he played with their son and daughter. Mr. Redding became like a surrogate father to Dan, and he felt like a member of their family.

The Reddings were always a pivotal part of his life as Dan grew older. They attended his graduations and spent holidays with him and his mother. Once Dan started a family of his own, Mr. and Mrs. Redding were like grandparents to his children, and the Reddings' children were like an aunt and uncle. Dan couldn't imagine his life without the Reddings, but his father and biological siblings couldn't understand his connection to them. For Dan, family consisted of his wife, his children, his mother, and the Redding family.

Family is not solely by blood; it's also
- The people who choose you
- The people you feel deeply connected to
- The people who lovingly hold you accountable

- The people who offer you a sense of safety
- The people who consistently show up for you
- The people who are willing to give you what you need
- The people who know you well and love you greatly

In adulthood, we choose our relationships. Family means connection, not just blood ties. Dan chose his family based on where he felt the most connected and supported.

Titles vs. Roles

People can hold a title without playing the role associated with that title. For instance, some mothers aren't nurturing, caring, or reassuring. Some siblings aren't loyal or supportive. Assuming someone embodies certain qualities based on their title is simply inaccurate. It's possible for a person to trust a friend more than a sibling, for example.

Ten Important Components of a Healthy Relationship
1. Trust
2. Joyful interactions
3. Deep (meaningful) conversations
4. Authenticity
5. Nurturing each other's needs
6. Healthy communication
7. Kindness (with considerate correction)
8. Appreciating each other
9. Providing comfort
10. Support (verbally and physically)

These components can be found in relationships within the family or with friends, elders, coworkers, mentors, neighbors, and so on.

Chosen Family

Believing that biological family is everything will keep you in unhealthy relationships because you think you have to tolerate anything. When people say, "I have a small family," they sometimes mean, "I have a small number of people with whom I choose to maintain relationships within my family. There are family members I speak to often, and some family members I don't talk with as often. The differences in frequency are primarily due to my choice, intentionally choosing where I want to spend my energy."

In some relationships, you may get most of what you need; and in others, maybe half of what you need. In still others, you may get little or nothing in return as you pour your energy into them. Healthy relationships are not fifty-fifty, as people do not contribute in all areas equally. Only you can decide if a relationship is worth it to you.

Only you can decide if a relationship is worth it to you.

While I was chatting with my therapist about a complex family relationship, she asked, "Why do you have a relationship with this person?" As a therapist, I knew the relationship was doomed because I didn't have a reason. I couldn't think of anything to say other than "because they're family." That isn't a valid reason to maintain a relationship, especially one that causes stress. Of course, there are times when people get on our nerves, yet we see value in the relationship. Be clear about when relationships have value and when they're simply an obligation.

Much like Dan, I grew up in a home with an older sibling, and after elementary school, I was the only child in the house. My deep connections occurred in friendships with peers, who, surprisingly, were the youngest in their families and had older siblings with significant age gaps. My family is well acquainted with my high school and early college friends because the relationships feel like sisterhoods. Like Dan's, many of my memories of celebrations are centered on some biological family and my chosen family.

Family is important, but the people you count as family are essential.

How to Support People with Unhealthy Family Relationships

Don't Minimize Their Experience

It isn't your job to tell someone "it's not that bad." Also, it isn't helpful to tell someone to push through difficult situations with family members. Allow people to choose what they want in their life.

Don't Push Them to Improve Their Relationships

You don't know what's best for other people because you can't be sure how certain relationships affect them. Unhealthy relationships can be detrimental to their mental health.

Allow Them Space to Share Without Judgment

Even when your story is different, it's essential to allow people to share their own stories.

Don't Tell Them What You Would Do If You Were in Their Shoes

Everyone's situation is different, so you can't always offer sound advice. Even if you would choose to react differently, people may not want to hear what you would do.

Don't Assume You Know How They Feel

Feelings are complicated, and you can't predict how someone might feel. If you come from a stable family, you won't have a reference point for someone with chaotic family relationships.

Don't Give Someone False Hope by Saying Things Like "It Will Work Out"

You don't know if it will work out; you can only assume and hope it will. It's OK not to know how things will play out.

Ask Them What They Need from You

Instead of assuming you know what someone needs, ask them what they need. This will ensure that their needs are met. Otherwise, you may keep yourself busy doing things they never asked you to do.

Supporting Yourself

When you don't have the support from blood or chosen family that you'd like, you can be for yourself what you wish others would be. You can teach yourself what you'd like others to teach you. What you're searching for in others lies within you. Supporting yourself looks like striving to be the best version of yourself and offering yourself grace along the way.

Five Ways to Support Yourself
Get to Know Yourself
As you learn more about yourself, you'll become more aware of your needs, desires, likes, and dislikes. Changing is a part of the process as well. Therefore, what you like may change from year to year. Knowing who you are helps you be clear with others about your preferences and needs.

Guided journals, workbooks, therapy, and meaningful conversations are wonderful ways to develop a deeper understanding of yourself. In therapy, I have wondered out loud the reason behind some of my choices, and I've given myself grace for not always making the best decisions.

Reduce Self-Neglect

Take impeccable care of yourself. Give yourself pep talks. Take warm baths. Go to the doctor regularly for checkups. We can't stop others from neglecting us, but we can stop ignoring ourselves.

Tanesha's mother didn't take her to the dentist during her childhood except when she was in crisis with a toothache or a chipped tooth. So she began to associate her trips to the dentist with pain. As she learned to take better care of herself, she began to go to the dentist as recommended for preventive care and maintenance, not only in a crisis.

Trust Yourself

You won't always make the best decisions, but the more of them you make, the better a decision-maker you will become. Avoiding decisions keeps you in limbo and doesn't improve your outcomes.

The key to trusting yourself is offering yourself grace when things don't go as planned, knowing that you acted in your best interests. Even some of the best decision-makers mess up from time to time. We see others as great decision-makers because we're unaware of how many times they've failed. As Nelson Mandela said, "Do not judge me by my successes, judge me by how many times I fell down and got back up again."

Focus on Your Needs

When taking care of others and operating in crisis have been the norm, it can be hard to unlearn the belief that taking care of others is more important than taking care of yourself. Your needs may not be more important than those of others, but yours are *most* important for yourself.

When my children were babies, I quickly learned that my ability to produce milk for them was directly tied to my ability to take care of myself. I had to nurture myself by resting, drinking enough water, and minimizing emotional distractions. In this way, mothering my babies taught me a few lessons about mothering myself. When you're operating at a deficit, you have a lot less to give.

Be Who You Need

It's a cliché, but it's true: sometimes, you can't find a person to fill a role, so you have to do the job yourself. Be the person you would have looked up to in childhood. Make yourself proud by becoming what you wish existed in your family.

Be the person you would have looked up to in childhood.

Building Community

Your family is just one part of your community, and you can be in community with many others who might provide what you need. If you grew up in a dysfunctional family, it might be hard to know who to trust. Trusting everyone can be unhealthy, but trusting no one is also unhealthy. It's advantageous to learn to discern whom you can trust.

Signs That It's Safe to Be Vulnerable
- You notice the other person is curious about your story.
- They are vulnerable with you.
- When they listen, you feel heard.
- They affirm you in the moment.

- They demonstrate integrity when they share other people's business.
- They consistently show up for you.

Vulnerability will lead you to authentic relationships. Show up as yourself, be honest and clear about your expectations, and you will find your community.

Keep the Connection Alive

Being in healthy relationships requires time and consistency. Maintain contact regularly over a period of time, and you will build healthy relationships. Waiting for the other person to reach out first might not help you stay connected in a manner that works for you. If you want a relationship, put your best foot forward, hoping that the other person does the same. Of course, not all relationships will work out. Let go of the ones that need to be released while being open to new ones. Expect some relationships to end; the best thing you can wish for is that they end without drama.

EXERCISE

Grab your journal or a piece of paper to complete the following prompts:

- ❋ Do you have any friends, neighbors, or mentors you view as family?
- ❋ How can you begin to foster deeper connections with people outside your biological family?

PART THREE
GROWING

CHAPTER 11

Troubleshooting Relationships with Parents

Anthony began therapy with me to work through his resentment toward his father, Michael. After having been absent in Anthony's life for twenty-two years, Michael wanted a relationship with his son. Anthony wondered if he wanted to reconnect with his father, who had remarried and fathered two children in his new family.

Anthony was fortunate enough to have a close relationship with his stepfather, who had been in his life since he was eight years old. His mother had moved on after Michael left, when Anthony was four years old. In some ways, reconnecting with his father felt like a betrayal to his stepfather, whom he considered his "real" father.

Throughout the years, Anthony had stayed in close contact with his paternal grandmother, and when she died, he saw Michael at the funeral, who asked him for his contact information. The initial conversations were slow, and Anthony wanted an apology. After two months of talking to his dad every other week, Anthony asked why he had stayed away and why he wanted a relationship now. Michael explained that he didn't know how to repair the issues between them and was sorry for his absence. But Anthony couldn't understand why his father would wait so long to try to make amends.

After talking to Michael for four months, Anthony stopped answering the calls and texts. He couldn't get past thinking, "Why now and not then?" He didn't feel like he needed his father as much as when he was a child. He didn't know how to feel angry and also open his heart to Michael.

In our work together, Anthony told me he wanted to "get over" being angry toward his father and figure out if he wanted a relationship. Since loyalty was valuable to him, he worried that building a relationship with Michael would adversely affect his bond with his stepfather.

"Getting Over" Your Feelings

Often, people seek therapy with the hope of getting over uncomfortable emotions, but you don't have to "get over" anything. Indeed, trying to get over hard feelings takes more energy than allowing yourself to be angry, hurt, or frustrated. Getting over it won't change the past. It's important to work through your feelings while moving forward in life.

People often say to me things like this:

> "My grandmother died. Can you help me get over it?"
> "I lost a job that I loved. I want to get over the pain and
>   embarrassment."
> "My best friend ghosted me, and I'm so sad. How do I get
>   over this?"

The truth is that no therapist, vice, or void-filler will help you get over emotions you're still processing. My typical response to people looking to "get over" something is, "I can help you feel better by allowing yourself to feel multiple emotions at once, validating your feelings, and helping you cope using healthy strategies." It isn't what people expect to hear, but it's the truth. Many times, I wish I had a "get over it" pill, but that doesn't exist. And there's nothing healthy that can stop you from feeling.

Anthony needed to be angry without seeing it as useless, bad, or even good. He needed to feel it without judgment. Anger gets a bad rap in our society, but there's nothing wrong with it. The challenge with anger is how we react and behave when we're angry. We have a tendency to focus on people who engage in destructive behavior when angry, but violence isn't the only reaction. I've seen people destroy property, and I've witnessed others go for a stroll.

Healthy Ways to Manage Anger

- Own it. Stop pretending you aren't angry and accept the feeling.
- Learn what triggers your anger—certain words, memories, environments, etc. You don't have to avoid being triggered, but you can plan how you want to respond when you know you're stirred up.
- Determine if it's worth it to put yourself in certain situations if you'll be triggered. Knowing your triggers will make it easier to decide what to do.
- Get to the core of your feelings. As Anthony processed his anger, he found that his core disappointment was a feeling of abandonment by his father. With anger, there's often underlying sadness, disappointment, or hurt.
- Develop strategies to express your anger that will help you let it go. Talking about your anger is helpful when you're intentional with your words. Relationships can benefit when the other person knows exactly how you feel. When you don't speak up, it still shows up in your behavior through passive-aggressive actions.

Denied anger turns into violence, passive-aggressiveness, depression, or hurtful words and behaviors. Anger isn't a problematic emotion; it's natural and needs to be acknowledged for it to subside. The best thing we can do is be honest with ourselves about our feelings.

Deciding to Stay and Work Through a Relationship or Leave

Anthony wanted to determine if he should pursue or reject the relationship with his father. This was a sign that he cared about figuring out the best possible solution for both himself and Michael.

To determine what's best, consider this:

- Is there abuse, or is the person dangerous?
- Does the offending party seem remorseful or willing to acknowledge their role in the relationship challenges?
- Is there one problem or many problems that need to be resolved?
- Has the person changed? What is the evidence of change?
- Will acknowledging the problem lead to change or more of the same destructive behaviors?
- What solutions have you tried in the past? If they weren't effective, was there an issue with your methods, or was the other person unwilling to participate?
- Can you live with ending the relationship?

In my years as a therapist, I've seen people maintain relationships with parents who were physically abusive in childhood but apologetic to their adult children. Conversely, I've seen people maintain relationships with parents who haven't changed and who refuse to acknowledge what they did was wrong or harmful. In all instances, it's everyone's choice to continue a relationship or not. Michael seemed to be remorseful, apologetic, and willing to take responsibility for the weight of his actions. Nevertheless, it's still up to Anthony to decide if the relationship with his father is worth pursuing.

How to Stop Hating Your Parents

You don't have to forgive and forget to stop being angry at your parents. Two things can exist: your truth about the relationship and your desire to maintain the relationship. You can accept your parents for who they are and how they treat you. What happened in your parent's life that shaped their relationship with you? There are no valid excuses for mistreating you. However, understanding breeds grace. They may have a history of trauma or addiction, or they may lack the skills necessary to nurture you. Their life experiences and unhealthy coping strategies likely affected you and your relationship with them. It isn't your fault, and you can't fix their issues. Step outside the situation and use your parent's first name (instead of "my mother's" or "my father's"): What is ____'s story? How did that story shape them?

Your parents are humans first, and as humans, they might

- Make mistakes
- Not apologize
- Be emotionally immature
- Struggle with keeping a promise
- Have unreasonable expectations

- Not have all the answers
- Be unaware of how they impact others
- Want things to go their way
- Cope in unhealthy ways
- Be unaware of what they don't know

What Are Your Parents' Stories?

Their stories aren't an excuse for what happened, but they're valuable information about the reasons for their behaviors. If your parent is unable to tell their story, ask other family members to share what they know. Children often bear the scars of their parent's trauma.

Things You May Be Waiting To Hear from Your Parents

- "I didn't have the tools to give you what you needed."
- "I was working through my stuff and didn't know how to raise you while healing."
- "I made mistakes and hurt you."
- "What can I do now to improve our relationship?"
- "I was overwhelmed, and it was reflected in my parenting."
- "I didn't know how to handle your emotions because I didn't know how to handle my own."
- "I did my best, but it wasn't what you needed."

Control What You Can

Focus on the parts of your relationship that you can control. Nurture the parts of yourself that need attention. Teach yourself what they didn't or couldn't teach you. While you may never turn your parents into what you want, you can acknowledge and enjoy the meaningful, warm, and healthy parts of your relationship with them.

Questions to Consider When Working Through Your Issues with Your Parents

- What is your definition of a healthy parent?
- How did your parent(s) show they loved you?
- What are some of the current issues in your relationship with your parent(s)?
- What expectations do you want to implement going forward in your relationship with your parent(s)?
- What do you need to accept about your parent(s) and your relationship with them?

Offer Them Grace

What are your flaws? What are your parents' flaws? Everyone has them, and it isn't always helpful to label one person's flaws as worse than someone else's. This doesn't mean that all is forgiven, but it's possible that your parent(s) didn't know how to manage the job of parenthood.

It Isn't Your Fault

Parents come with their own history. Marcy's mother abused her verbally and physically, while her mom's boyfriend abused her sexually. Although Marcy didn't grow up to abuse her own children, she still had an alcohol problem, just like her mother. Both Marcy and her mother experienced trauma. This isn't an excuse, but it's an explanation of what happened to them.

In a perfect world, parents would have children only after they've done substantial work on themselves. It's unlikely that everyone will be healed and whole before becoming parents, and many deal with their own difficult issues while they raise their children. As discussed in Chapter 3, a parent's substance issue is never a child's fault.

Talk About the Problems

It's hard to leave the past in the past if you're still haunted by what happened, and it's harmful to constantly bring up issues from the past. Still, your parents could benefit from knowing how you feel about how they parented you. Open communication is a healthy part of any relationship, but how you communicate matters.

It can be intimidating to have an overdue conversation about painful memories, but putting it off will only increase your anxiety. It's true that you can't control how they'll respond, but knowing your parents as you do, you might be able to predict their reaction. Despite whatever happened in the past, speak up if you have something new or different to say.

Ways to Express Your Grievances

Tell them how much you value the relationship; then, tell them what you need them to know and your expectations from sharing the information.

> Example: "This relationship is important to me, and I need you to know that when I was younger, I felt that you were often too preoccupied to spend time with me. I know there's nothing you can do about that now, but I wanted to release it."

> "I love you, and I have something important to say. You yell at me when you're frustrated, and it's something that has been happening for some time now. In the future, when you yell, I will bring it to your attention and will return to the conversation only when things are calmer."

Write your parents a letter to let them know how you feel. Letter writing is a pathway to releasing your emotions without a confrontation. You may opt to share the letter with your parents or keep it to yourself as simply an emotional release.

Writing your thoughts and feelings on paper can be a cathartic process. Type them on your computer or create a note on your phone if that's easier for you. The letter should include a statement of the issues, how you were/are affected, how you feel, and the next steps you envision. But focus on the big problem rather than tackling every issue at once.

If you decide to share your letter with your parents, determine if you want to mail it, email it, or give it to them in person. Bear in mind that they may not respond at all or in a way you find appropriate. I've even heard of some parents reading the letter and never mentioning that it was received because they aren't ready to have a conversation. If you want to ensure that your letter was seen and the contents were digested, ask them directly, "When you saw my letter, what did you think about it?"

Talking through issues as they happen is the gold standard for communicating in relationships. But once you've cleared the air, make it a point to not bring up the problems constantly. Again, you don't have to forgive and forget, but do move forward. Whenever possible, talk about problems as they happen or soon after.

Talking about issues as they happen might sound like:

- "You're dismissing my feelings when you say things like 'It's not that bad.'"
- "Don't call me names when you're upset."
- "Please stop playing games on your phone while I'm trying to talk to you."

Talking about issues soon after they happen might sound like:

- "Yesterday, while we were talking, you dismissed my feelings by saying things like 'It's not that bad.'"
- "Last week, when we were having a discussion, you called me a derogatory name."
- "A few days ago, while we were talking, you kept playing with your phone."

Many of us were led to believe it's disrespectful to talk about problems. But as hard as it may be to do, it's worth it. You aren't under a deadline, however, so prepare yourself for tough conversations without putting them off too long. Sad to say, there is no easy or perfect time. Have the conversations soon, because in the process of delaying, you will continue to suffer.

Set Clear Boundaries

You deserve boundaries now, and you did as a kid, too. In dysfunctional families, boundaries are viewed as a threat to the overall system. Asking for something different, expressing an expectation, or not going along with the typical chaos can all seem like you're trying to make waves in the family. The truth is that you *are* making waves because you're refusing to continue in dysfunction.

In healthy relationships, boundaries aren't offensive. Even when people don't like your boundaries, they can respect them. Liking the boundary is optional; respecting the boundary is nonnegotiable.

Boundaries in dysfunctional families might sound like:

- "Mom, your brother isn't invited to my house."
- "I'm not giving you money to buy drugs."

- "Stop bringing up religion to condone being physically abusive."
- "Making fun of my weight is not funny to me. Stop."

How to Manage When You're Dependent

If you're dependent on your parents for financial support, there's a potential for harm if you're honest with them. For children, teens, or adults who have moved back home or never left home, here are some ways to manage the family issues:

Find support outside the family
>Talk to a trusted peer, mental health professional, or family member who can support you. Don't struggle alone.

Plan your exit strategy
>Attend school to finish your education or gain new skills. Work and save to move out.

Resist being stuck
>Develop a healthy mentality and focus your sights on becoming independent.

How to Manage Being a Caregiver to Your Parents

When you can let go of what you need from your parents and allow them to be who they are, your relationship can transform into a more authentic experience. Some things don't get better with time, however. We rarely talk about how hard it is to accept that our parents were never what we needed in childhood and still aren't what we need. Even though we can't change people, it can be difficult to have relationships with those who won't change. Give yourself a lot of grace if you're still accepting the reality of who your parents are.

Roles are reversed when children provide financial support to able-bodied, financially inept, or irresponsible parents, or when they provide emotional support or physically care for a parent. In these situations, adult children support themselves and their own family as well as their parents. This can breed resentment and frustration.

It's your choice to help your parents or allow them to resolve their own problems.

To manage financial support of a parent, it might be helpful to

- Decide on an amount, sort of like an allowance, that works within your budget
- Say no when you can't afford to help
- Offer to connect them to a financial counselor
- Consider taking over their spending as a conservator

To manage emotional support of a parent, it might be helpful to

- Let them know which topics you're uncomfortable discussing
- Encourage them to build a social network with peers or family members in their age range
- Let them know how hearing certain things makes you feel
- Redirect the conversation when it moves toward uncomfortable territory
- Suggest that your parent talk to a therapist

To manage caring for a parent's physical needs, it might be helpful to

- Speak with their insurance company, connecting with a case manager to find out what's available through the policy
- Ask other family members for support instead of shouldering everything on your own
- Build a support system to process the mental stress of caring for a parent

Raising Your Parents

Children want to be guided with structure and expectations. When the child is the mature one in the relationship, it can be hard to take parents seriously.

For years, Amy expected her mother to "grow up." On holidays, her mom would cuss out family members and struggle to maintain her composure in public spaces. Amy saw her mother as immature and wanted her to "act her age." But physical age doesn't determine psychological maturity.

How to Manage Your Relationship with Emotionally Immature Parents

- Determine their emotional age, as opposed to their chronological age, and set your expectations accordingly. Your parents may not resemble the other parents in their age bracket.
- Don't compare them with their peers. Consider their history and compare them with their previous behavior. Most people will continue to be who they've been in the past.
- State the problem and be clear (repeatedly) about your expectations. Don't get caught up in their reaction to the issues. You can't change how they respond.

Parents with Unmanaged Mental Health Issues

It can be challenging to have a relationship with someone who denies their issues and won't consider mental health treatment. Depression, anxiety, personality, and other mental health problems impact parent-child relationships. Some people may never accept a diagnosis that has been given or symptoms that lead to a diagnosis. A person may exhibit mental health symptoms worthy of clinical diagnosis and never choose to receive care. When a family member refuses mental health treatment or denies having any issues, you can't force them to receive care. When someone is harmful to themselves or others, it is possible to solicit support from social or legal systems to intervene and ensure your loved one stays safe and doesn't harm others.

Jim's father had terrible mood swings, anger outbursts, and night terrors. But even when he was diagnosed with PTSD, he refused to seek treatment.

How to Manage Your Relationship with Parents with Unmanaged Mental Health Issues

- Step away from situations that become violent or abusive. A mental health issue doesn't give someone license to verbally or physically assault you.
- Give them space when they request it or start to seem distant.
- Create an emergency plan. This can be particularly helpful with family members who experience depression, bipolar disorder, or schizophrenia. The emergency plan should include triggering behaviors, who to contact in case of an emergency (including doctors and the nearby hospital), insurance information, and action steps to take. Key family members and stakeholders should be given a copy of this plan.

One-Sided Relationships with Parents

Riley calls her mother, Alice, once a week. But her mom rarely asks, "How are you doing?" and quickly returns to talking about herself if the topic turns to Riley's life.

While Riley wants to know what's happening with her mother, she doesn't want the entire conversation to be about Alice's life and complaints. She also wants her mother to sometimes initiate phone calls rather than having to always do it herself.

How to Manage One-Sided Relationships with Parents

- Insist on talking about yourself. Your parents can't dominate the conversation; it's OK to insert yourself.
- Let them know what you're experiencing.
- Redirect the conversation when it veers off track.

Letting them know what you feel might sound like:

- "When we talk, I'd like you to ask me more about what's happening in *my* world."
- "You seem engaged when we talk, and I'd like to hear from you more often. Please call me once a week."

Handling the interaction might look like:

- It might be troubling to talk multiple times a week to someone who centers the conversation on themselves. You aren't obligated to speak to them more often than feels comfortable for you.

- Your parents likely believe you're an excellent listener, or they have no one else to talk to. Accept that when you converse with them, your job is to listen, not to do anything about their problems.
- Encourage them to find support from others. You don't want to be the only person who listens to them.

Reparenting

Give yourself what you didn't have growing up. Some parents aren't emotionally equipped to meet your expectations, and they may never rise to the job of parenting in the way you'd like. In these instances, it's imperative that you parent yourself. Reparenting is a healthy way to nurture your inner child while offering yourself the care you needed.

Reparenting yourself can look like:

- Saying "I'm proud of you" to yourself
- Preparing nutritious meals for yourself
- Completing tasks slowly
- Reassuring yourself
- Planning celebrations for yourself
- Affirming yourself using "I am" statements, such as "I am adorable when my dimples show"
- Sleeping eight hours each night (and giving yourself a bedtime)
- Playing
- Rewarding yourself for big and small accomplishments

The Importance of Self-Care

Taking care of your emotional and physical needs should take precedence when you're from a dysfunctional family. An outlet like therapy can be an excellent way to support yourself, along with nurturing healthy relationships with other people in your life.

Changing your parents may not be possible, but changing how you show up in the relationship is within your control. When you desire to maintain contact, it's crucial to discern how to do so without harming yourself.

After draining interactions with family, allow yourself time to recover and determine how you want to engage moving forward. When a new issue presents itself, decide how you want to respond in the moment, or come back with a solution later. But don't let problems fester; address them as soon as possible.

EXERCISE

Grab your journal or a piece of paper to complete the following prompts:

* What are the main challenges in your relationship with your parent(s)?
* Do you know your parents' stories?
* How do you nurture yourself in ways your parents didn't?

CHAPTER 12

Troubleshooting Relationships with Siblings

Sierra and Sylvester were raised in a two-parent household. Because she was three years older, Sierra always felt that Sylvester was babied and given a pass for multiple screwups. Whenever she needed help, she didn't go to her parents, because they raised her to be independent and responsible. But they raised Sylvester in the opposite way—to be dependent and unreliable.

Sierra often wondered how the two of them could be so different, despite growing up in the same household. In private conversations, their father, William, acknowledged that Sylvester "had some growing up to do" and that their mother, Sonya, had enabled Sylvester's dependency. Sonya was tied at the hip to her son and refused to admit that she'd treated her children differently.

Unconsciously, Sierra took out her frustrations toward her parents on Sylvester. She was short with him, found him annoying, and refused to speak to him except at family gatherings. She cited the following differences in treatment by her parents:

- Sylvester was given a brand-new car when he turned sixteen, while Sierra was given a used car when she turned eighteen.

- Sierra was encouraged to go to college in state to reduce costs. Meanwhile, Sylvester was allowed to attend college out of state.
- Sierra graduated from college with honors in four years and threw herself a celebration. When Sylvester graduated in six years, their parents planned his party.
- After college, Sierra moved to another state for work and raised her children with her husband. Her parents visited once a year, but when Sylvester had kids, they watched his two children nearly every weekend. Despite this being due to proximity, Sierra was jealous.

Sierra watched for signs of mistreatment and kept score, always feeling she was on the losing side. She found it hard not to be mad at her brother. While it mostly wasn't his fault, he never stood up for his sister or fought for her to get equal treatment. He gleefully accepted all the help he received from their parents.

Now forty years old, Sierra sought therapy to work through the years of resentment she'd harbored toward her family. Our work centered on building a relationship with her brother that was based on shared interests and a genuine connection. We couldn't make her parents acknowledge how they impacted the sibling dynamic, but we could help Sierra advocate for herself by asking her parents to meet her unique needs. In some instances, she didn't need precisely what was offered to her brother. She needed to discover how her parents could support her in a way that was meaningful to her as an individual.

How Parents Harm Sibling Relationships

Parents aren't solely responsible for sibling relationships, but what they do or don't do can significantly affect the dynamic between brothers and sisters. Most parents will say they went through a phase in which their children bickered over almost everything. I've heard parents say things like, "I'm not getting in the middle of it; figure it out," or "It's your brother; you have to share with him." These statements do very little to eliminate bickering and may even lead to more sibling conflict.

In this chapter, I'll provide advice to parents as well as to those struggling through difficult sibling relationships as adults.

Choosing or Not Choosing Sides

There are times when arguing siblings are harmful toward each other. For example, when one child is playing with a toy and the other child snatches the toy from them.

> *In this situation, it's appropriate for a parent to say something like this:*
> "Your sister was playing with the toy. If you want to play with it, wait until she's finished, or ask her for the toy."

Even though children won't always follow this request, it sends the message that certain behaviors aren't acceptable.

> *It isn't appropriate for a parent to say something like this:*
> "I'm staying out of it. You need to figure it out on your own."

Figuring it out on their own is what prompted the children to fight over the toy in the first place. Kids need to be reminded (repeatedly) of how to treat others, mainly when they're younger and struggle with empathy. With teenagers and grown children, it makes sense to work through solutions with them.

Example: Your daughter calls to vent about her sister borrowing money for a car repair and not paying her back.

It's appropriate for a parent to say something like this:
    "I hear she committed to paying you back, and she didn't keep her promise. How will you address this with her?"

As a parent, you don't have to get in the middle of disputes between adult children, but you also shouldn't condone behavior you genuinely feel is unacceptable.

It isn't appropriate for a parent to say something like this:
    "She needs the money more than you, so why not just let her have it?"

It may be true that one sister has less money than the other, but no one should feel pressured or obligated to loan money to anyone else.

Favoring One Child over Another

Sierra saw her brother as the "favorite" child. Sylvester didn't choose this designation for himself, but he was given it by his parents, for reasons outside his control. Perhaps they treated him differently because he's the youngest, he's a male, he's easier to get along with, or he reminds their mother of herself. It's uncomfortable for parents to face that they haven't been fair, so many will deny it when it takes place.

It's appropriate for a parent to say something like this:
    "You're right. We purchased your brother a new car because we were financially able to do so. I understand how frustrating it might be to see him being treated differently in that way."

It isn't appropriate for a parent to say something like this:
> "That was years ago. Your car was as good as his. Be grateful
> for what you were given."

Parents usually treat kids differently, and it's OK to admit it. Everyone's needs and interests are different, so it's difficult to always be 100 percent fair or equal. Still, denying unfair treatment doesn't help the situation; it diminishes trust between parent and child. When parents are honest about unequal treatment, it can help the offended child feel more connected to them.

Forcing "Love" and Positive Feelings

Despite blood ties, there may be few emotional ties between siblings. This is especially common when they're raised in different homes, have little in common, have an age gap, express different views about family dysfunction, or have significantly different personalities. Love happens naturally, so parents can't force their children to love each other.

To build connection, some parents force their children to speak positively about one another and push through relationship challenges even after one has hurt the other deeply. It might be hard for a parent to listen to one child speak negatively about another, but parents should acknowledge their children's concerns. Creating space for them to express their feelings will help them feel less alone and more connected to their parents.

It's appropriate for a parent to say something like this:
> "I hear you saying you don't feel connected to your brother
> because he's younger than you, and there isn't much you have
> in common."

It isn't appropriate for a parent to say something like this:
     "Your brother and sisters are your family no matter what,
and you have to love them because they're all you have."

Comparing

It's easy to fall into the comparison trap, but people can be different without being compared with each other. Sometimes, parents think it's harmless to make comparisons between siblings, but it can be hurtful to the relationships between their children, especially when a child notices that their brother or sister is favored. The child may then indirectly ask for the same treatment. For instance, the child might say, "You said her hair was pretty. Is my hair pretty, too?" Since children are different, it makes sense to compliment them for different things. Lying to create equality by saying "I like your hair, too" won't be seen as genuine. So, when you issue one compliment, be ready to issue multiples. In short, don't ever compare your children with their siblings.

For example, avoid saying things like, "When your brother was five years old, he could tie his shoe. Why can't you?" Don't allow your children to see themselves as deficient because they haven't achieved something within the same time frame as another child in the family. This continues to apply once children have reached adulthood.

It's appropriate for a parent to say something like this:
     "I'm willing to help you with your rent this month."

It isn't appropriate for a parent to say something like this:
     "Your brother never asks me for help with his rent. Why
can't you be more independent like him?"

Gossiping About One Child to Another

Parents may get frustrated with a child and need an outlet for that frustration, but when that outlet is a sibling in the family, it can create big problems. Airing your differences will no doubt put the confidant child in the middle. They may then feel the need to fix the situation, or they may make the situation worse by expressing their own grievances.

Gossiping means

- Attempting to tear down someone's character
- Discussing secondhand information as if it's factual
- Exaggerating to make a person or situation seem worse than it is
- Repeating a narrative that isn't true
- Sharing things that are harmful for others to know
- Spreading assumptions
- Sensationalizing details
- Revealing someone else's secrets

Nevertheless, research suggests that talking through your frustrations provides social and psychological connections. With parent-to-child gossip, it's essential to ensure that the shared information isn't salacious or intended to harm. Parents should air such grievances only with adult children who have a solid understanding of the situation and a mutual desire to improve it. Also, the information shared should be based solely on facts.

It's appropriate for a parent to say something like this:
    "I'm concerned about your sister. She seems more withdrawn since she started dating her new girlfriend."

It isn't appropriate for a parent to say something like this:
> "Your sister isn't ready to date, and I don't like her new girl-friend. Did you know they met at work? I can't believe she's dating someone she works with. How sloppy!"

Denying Problems

When parents have a codependent relationship with one child, it impacts the sibling relationships. For example, Erica graduated from college and was financially independent, yet her parents seemed to focus most of their energy on her younger sister, who had multiple legal convictions and always needed financial help. Their parents always praised Erica's sister for even the most minor thing, such as getting a job. Meanwhile, Erica was gainfully employed, but her parents didn't seem to regard her accomplishments in the same way.

It's appropriate for a parent to say something like this:
> "It's true; we help your sister financially because we don't think she'd be able to function without our financial support."

It isn't appropriate for a parent to say something like this:
> "We treat both of our children the same."

Siblings Parenting Siblings

Sometimes, parents place the role of parenting on older, more emotionally mature, or seemingly capable siblings.

Siblings taking on parental roles might happen under the following circumstances:

- When a parent works and older siblings are used as childcare providers for younger siblings

- If a parent has substance use problems and the oldest child takes care of younger siblings
- If a parent is sick and the older sibling cares for younger siblings

When this happens, the caregiving sibling may start to resent their brothers and sisters, or they may find it hard to relinquish the caregiver role, even when their siblings enter adulthood. I've heard people say, for example, "My sister was my mother." These dynamics leave little room for true, healthy sibling relationships to develop.

However, when an older child has raised the other children through no fault of their own, it's possible to shift the relationship dynamics when the issue is acknowledged in adulthood. The caregiving sibling can begin to provide resources instead of completing tasks and encourage their brother or sister to care for themselves. It helps to be open about the role reversal that has taken place.

Common Challenges in Adult Sibling Relationships

Siblings who have issues with each other in adulthood typically experience envy, resentment, one-sided relationships, betrayal, incongruent beliefs, and differing lifestyles. From childhood to adulthood, however, many siblings learn to resolve disputes, accept each other, and develop mutual support.

These are common issues reported in one of my online surveys:

- "My mother raised my half-sibling and wasn't present for me."
- "My parent favors my sibling, as evidenced by spending more time with them and giving them extravagant gifts."
- "My siblings assume I'm the favorite."

- "My siblings still treat me like a child."
- "My sibling has a severe drug problem, and my parents support them."
- "My sibling takes advantage of my parents."
- "My sibling bullied me and still makes fun of me."
- "My mom has manipulated all five of her children against each other, and now we don't get along."

In addition to such challenges, these issues also tend to plague sibling relationships:

- Fights over inheritance
- Disputes about taking care of parents
- Clashing political views
- Severe bullying in the relationship during childhood
- A history of physical and sexual abuse

Every Child in the Family Is Impacted by Dysfunction

In dysfunctional families, each child may play a specific role. Here are some of the roles that children within a family may take on unconsciously.

The Responsible One

This child takes care of problems by managing crises, paying bills, setting rules, and ensuring the care of everyone in the family. They deeply need structure and create it for themselves when parents do not. Self-reliance becomes a way of being, as this child understands that others aren't dependable.

The Placater

This child is known as the sensitive one who believes they show and say how they feel. They often try to help others with their emotions and take on the burden of managing chaotic moments. They don't draw attention to themselves, but instead feel the pain of others and try to lessen that pain.

The Hero

This child appears to be successful and emotionally stable. People presume they come from a healthy family dynamic because they have no outward appearance of dysfunction. But this person often struggles with anxiety and developing emotional attachments due to underlying shame and a history of emotional neglect from their family.

The Mascot

This child helps cover up family problems by keeping everyone entertained. They have a pattern of masking problems, deflecting emotions, and detaching emotionally from their environment. They grow up feeling uncomfortable with admitting or naming what they feel, and they often see themselves as responsible for other people's feelings even in adulthood.

The Adjuster/Adapter

This child tries to stay quiet and out of the way, adapting to almost any circumstance without complaint. They go along with whatever is happening in the environment and refuse to draw attention to themselves. Consequently, they have many unmet needs and come to believe that others can't or won't meet those needs. Since they've grown up disconnecting from themselves and others, this child struggles with developing intimate relationships in adulthood.

The "Acting Out" Child (Scapegoat)

This child is often blamed for the problems in the family. They demonstrate the family's dysfunction via behaviors such as stealing, substance misuse, lying, fighting, or anything that draws attention to themselves. Their behaviors bring awareness to problems within the family.

Healing Sibling Relationships

If you're struggling in a relationship with one or more of your siblings, consider these strategies.

Acceptance

Meet them where they are, and don't push them. Perhaps your sibling is struggling with substance misuse or has a lifestyle that you don't quite understand. You can't change those things about them, and trying to convince them to be anything else will just push them away.

You can get along with a sibling who has an entirely different personality from yours, but you must accept your differences, including the aspects that you consider to be less than ideal. For example, Marie's brother Carter was diagnosed with bipolar disorder in his early twenties. His behavior was unpredictable and concerning at times. Marie didn't feel comfortable having him at her house, but she felt she could meet him for lunch once a month at one of his favorite diners. It wasn't the type of relationship she'd always wanted, but it was what she could manage.

Emotional Maturity

For the sake of your peace, release the need to control what your sibling does or doesn't do. You can only control how you respond. Don't be surprised when they demonstrate who they are. In therapy, people arrive with a load of issues related to people who aren't in the treatment space with them. Those people aren't seeking help, or they might be seeking help but aren't in the room, so the goal isn't to change them. Instead, the goal is for the person seeking therapy to explore their own feelings, change the way they react, and relax their expectations.

Grace and Compassion

Grammy-winning gospel artist Kirk Franklin shared this story: *Two boys were raised by their alcoholic father. One son grew up and followed in his father's footsteps; he, too, became an alcoholic. When asked what happened, he answered, "I watched my father." The other son grew up and did not use alcohol. When asked what happened, he answered, "I watched my father." Same household, same experiences, and two different perspectives.*

You can live through the same experiences as your sibling and have a completely different perspective and takeaway. Personality, temperament, mental and emotional health, and genetics determine your mindset. If you see your sibling as a unique individual, it might be easier to develop compassion for who they are, no matter the path they've chosen.

Unpacking Resentment

Resentment can build and reach a point where you find it challenging to engage with your siblings. It's essential to acknowledge, name, and feel whatever emotions you have. There is no need to shame yourself for being upset about incidents in the past. You not imagining things, and you aren't being mean. Feel what you feel without judgment so that you don't take your emotions out on others.

If you tell your sibling what you've been feeling, you might give them some insight that helps them see your perspective. No one can correct the past, but acknowledging your wounds can help heal your relationship now and improve future interactions.

Acknowledging your resentment might sound like:

- "Mom seemed to favor boys. Therefore, I felt like she was harder on me and gave you fewer consequences."
- "You were able to stand up for yourself in a way that I never felt comfortable doing, and our parents seemed to listen when you did."
- "You seemed unfazed by the fact that our parents were addicts. You were able to make friends and do well in school, and I couldn't with everything happening at home."
- "When we were younger, Mom always made me take you with me wherever I went. So I was mean to you then, and sometimes, I still get upset by how Mom puts me in a position to take care of you."
- "Dad treated you as if you were the special 'Daddy's little girl,' and he was harder on me. For years, I ignored you because I didn't want to be another person treating you like a princess."

Moving Through the Discomfort of Openness

You can control your delivery, but you can't control how someone will respond. It makes sense to fear that your sibling might overreact or become defensive. However, consider the possibility that speaking up might make things better between you. Be clear that you're being honest about the challenges you've had with them because you want to improve the relationship and make it work. If your sibling becomes defensive, let them speak, because chances are, they're shocked by the revelations, no matter how true and self-evident they might feel to you. Don't deny their experience while owning your experience.

Six Ways to Protect Your Peace in Your Sibling Relationships

- Keep It Short

     Determine how long you can engage with your sibling before losing your patience or peace. What is the optimal amount of time for engagement? How long does it take before you feel dysregulated?

- Avoid Heated Conversations

     There are topics you won't discuss with your siblings. Which ones are off-limits? How long should you listen before changing the subject?

- Share Only What's Comfortable for You

     You can share based on your desire for your sibling to know more about you, but you don't have to say anything before you're ready.

     If someone asks you a question you're not ready to answer, practice saying something like this:

     "I'm not ready to share yet."

     "I'm still processing and not ready to talk about it."

     "I hear that you're concerned; I will let you know more when I'm ready to share."

- Spend Time Bonding

     In some instances, quality time is better than quantity time. You don't have to see each other often to feel connected. Don't force yourself to spend more time together than you want. Instead, find an activity you're both likely to enjoy. Perhaps there's a TV show you both like to watch, or it could be fun to try a new restaurant.

- Honor Each Other's Differences

    It's OK to be different, and it's important to embrace your differences. When you choose to be with other people, embrace who they are in those moments when you're spending time together and when you're apart. Loving someone can mean accepting their uniqueness.

- Place Boundaries, and Stick to Them

    Relationships need boundaries. Yours are your responsibility, and when you set one, it's your job to ensure it's honored. For example, if you inform your brother that he can't borrow more money until he pays you back what he already owes you, tell him no every time he asks for more. You can't make him stop asking, but you can be firm about your boundary.

Parenting Children Who Are Estranged from Each Other

Regardless of their age, it's hard to see your children not get along. When they're under your care, you can help them with their relationship. However, once they become adults, it's no longer your job. Even though you want your adult children to get along, meddling in their relationships can cause more issues.

I heard a story of a man who always had a contentious relationship with his brother. His parents would encourage him to "be nice" or "love your brother no matter what." He always felt like his brother was jealous of him and picked fights. After his mother died, he found a note his mother wrote that validated his concerns. His mother admitted to seeing how his brother was envious and petty, and she could not describe why this might be the case. The man felt relieved that his mother finally acknowledged his concerns.

When Your Children Are Estranged, Do This:

- Respect the boundaries that have been outlined, or specifically
  ask, "What do you want me to do or not do as the parent in this
  situation?"

Your children might set the following boundaries:

- "If my brother is coming to the gathering, please let me know, and
  I won't attend."
- "Please don't share anything about me with them."
- "I don't want to hear updates on what's happening with them."
- Don't try to force your kids to talk. Don't guilt-trip them by saying
  things like, "What will happen when I die?" or "All I want is for you
  to get along." Convincing your children to communicate isn't
  healthy for them, even if it makes you feel better. Relationships are
  only healthy when they're by choice.
- Deal with the discomfort of estranged children by talking to a
  therapist or trusted friend. Don't bury grief; work through it.
- Remain neutral and try to understand both sides.

Reminders About Sibling Relationships

- You might not be best friends with your siblings.
- You can have sibling rivalry as adults.
- Your parents may have contributed to your relationship issues
  with your siblings.
- You might not like your siblings' personalities.

With all of the above, if you choose, you can work through your challenges and have a relationship with your siblings.

EXERCISE

Grab your journal or a piece of paper to complete the following prompts:

* What are the top three issues in your relationships with your siblings?
* What can you do to be more at ease in your interactions?

CHAPTER 13

Troubleshooting Relationships
with Children

It had been two years since Chris last spoke to his daughter, London. Following his divorce from his ex-wife of twenty-one years, he tried to remain present in London's life, but she was always busy whenever he wanted to get together. When they did spend time together, she was moody and withdrawn. He knew the divorce had impacted his relationship with London, but he couldn't believe two years had passed without their talking or seeing each other.

London was always a daddy's little girl. She was twelve years old when the conflict in his marriage started to increase, and London took her mother's side. Her brother, Lance, was five years younger and seemed neutral. Lance had been able to maintain a relationship with both parents and even chose to live with Chris following the divorce.

London came home for breaks from college and made no attempts to see Chris. It hurt. When he started dating, London said terrible things about the woman he was seeing and spoke out about how her mother was treated. One day, London stopped responding to her father's calls. After a few attempts, Chris gave up trying to force the relationship. He even missed her graduation, and he didn't know where she lived or worked. He missed her deeply and didn't know how to repair the relationship or if it was even possible.

Chris was ashamed to talk about this with anyone. In therapy, he presented as guarded about what could've caused the collapse in his relationship with London. He blamed his ex-wife for most issues, saying, "She makes me look like a monster" or "She poisoned London against me." Meanwhile, he had a good relationship with Lance. They spoke by phone at least once a week, texted often, and traveled together occasionally. Lance preferred to stay out of the conflict, however, so he didn't mention his sister. Chris knew that Lance talked to her, but he chose not to pry because he feared messing up his relationship with Lance. So he often walked on eggshells around his son.

Chris sought therapy for anxiety. It took some time for him to open up about feeling responsible, sad, and scared about possibly never talking to his daughter again. To move through his anxiety, he had to become comfortable with naming his emotions, practicing self-compassion, and acknowledging what he'd done to create the situation. Then, he could determine how to move forward.

Accountability Matters

Sometimes, you're responsible for the problem, and it can be hard to admit what you did or didn't do to cause conflict with your child. Acknowledging the truth, however, can save your relationship.

We tend to repeat behaviors based on how we were raised. As a result, many of us don't learn to be the type of parent we want to be. It's essential to become clear about what we want to do differently with our own children.

Ultimately, your children will decide how you did as a parent, not you.

Parents might feel, "I did everything for them," while their child might feel, "My parents were never there for me." Perhaps both things are true, but the incongruency in these realities must be explored, not denied. In all likelihood, the parent was present in ways they deemed important but not in ways the child felt were needed.

Examples of Incongruent Experiences

Parent: "I was a single parent who worked hard to make sure our needs were met."

Child: "My mother never came to my games."

Parent: "My parents never talked to me about anything, and I wanted my kids to know the truth about everything."

Child: "My parents told me things prematurely, before I was prepared to handle them."

Parent: "I had an addiction. I couldn't take care of myself, let alone properly take care of my child."

Child: "My father was an addict, and now that he's clean, he expects instant forgiveness."

Parent: "My child had a great childhood. I always made sure they were happy."

Child: "My parents didn't ask me how I felt. They told me how to feel. It was important to them that I *appear* happy. Whenever I seemed to be displeased, they called me a brat."

Even when your intentions are not to cause harm, you may inadvertently harm your child. To recover, it's important to own your role in the harm, whether it was intentional or unintentional.

Common Errors Parents Make When Their Children Are Young

Lying to a child

If you want your children to be honest with you, be honest with them. Establish trust early in an age-appropriate manner.

Not admitting that you, too, can be wrong

Parents are often wrong, and many fail when they don't admit it. If you want children to be accountable, practice being accountable. Kids are like sponges—they absorb your behaviors, good and bad.

Parenting every child the same way

Each child is different and will require something different from you. You can't parent two different people in the same way. Get to know your children, and parent each of them according to their unique needs.

Blaming a child for things that weren't their responsibility

Children are often put in positions they can't manage and held responsible when something goes wrong. For example, Nevaeh wanted to pay for her senior trip, but her mother requested money from her for the electricity bill. When Nevaeh chose to use her funds for her trip, the electricity was disconnected, and her mother blamed her.

Early Bonding

Both mothers and fathers benefit from forming early attachments to their children. When parents live separately, the bond with the parent who lives outside the home can be hindered. Mental health, substance misuse, and the relationship parents have with each other can all affect the initial bond between parents and children. If a parent is emotionally detached, withdrawn, or struggling, those issues can harm the parent-child bond. How we start isn't how we have to finish, but some parents find it difficult to recover from this early damage, which may continue into adulthood.

Jessica was conceived after her mother had a few casual encounters. When her father found out about the pregnancy, he agreed to be present, but then he moved to another state after she was born. Whenever Jessica visited with her father, she felt as though she were in the company of a stranger. The relationship felt awkward, and she struggled to force a connection.

It's possible to stay connected to a child who lives in a separate home, but the parent must make an effort to stay involved in the child's day-to-day life. Close relationships are built over time. If parents want a close relationship with their adult children, it's important to build the foundation early.

Divorce and Breakups Change Relationships for Both Young and Adult Children

Even if a parental breakup happens when the child is an adult, it's usually painful. I include breakups with nonbiological parents because children become attached to stepparents and significant others who played a role in their life.

As a parent, you play a crucial role in how your breakups are handled. The best practice is for both partners to discuss the ending of the relationship with the children, reassuring them that it isn't their fault and talking about how the family will function going forward.

A child typically experiences trauma after breakups for the following reasons.

The Parents Are Grieving and Become More Withdrawn

When a parent goes through a breakup, they may retreat from the family. However, children continue to need parenting despite what their parents might be experiencing mentally and emotionally.

The Parent Becomes Angry at Their Ex

The hope is that all partnerships will last, but when they don't, some parties become angry toward the other. Leaving a partner doesn't necessarily mean leaving a child, however. Children (both young and adult) are often placed in the middle of parental disputes. In some cases, parents vent their frustrations about their partner, trying to intentionally push the child to take sides. Children of any age are not a healthy emotional outlet for a parent's relationship frustrations.

Parents must take care not to let their feeling about their ex corrupt the feelings of their child. A parent's anger can often get in the way of the child's relationship with the shunned partner, which can be very harmful for the child. I commonly see adult children struggle emotionally when their parents have to be in the same room together. When a parent is hurting, it can be hard to contain those feelings, and yet it is necessary for the children to have healthy relationships with their parents despite the co-parenting issues.

The Parents Lean Too Much on the Children for Emotional Support

Children are not emotionally equipped to handle their feelings around a parent's relationship with the other parent. When a partner has been abusive to both the parent and the child, however, sharing about those experiences may help a child feel less alone.

Harmful disclosures might sound like:

"Your mother is a slut, and she cheated on me throughout our
    entire relationship."
"Your father doesn't consider anyone but himself."
"Your mother is lazy and won't ever figure her life out."

Helpful disclosures might sound like:

"I can see how your mother's relationships impact you."
"It can be challenging to talk to your dad, and I wonder if he
    knows that about himself."
"I, too, hope that she figures out what's next."

The Family's Financial Resources Shift

Post-breakup, financial shifts may be uncontrollable, and this financial insecurity can affect a child's sense of safety. Families might need to move into a smaller space or stay with relatives, or a parent might need financial support from their adult child. These significant changes can be yet another unintended result of a breakup—one that affects the whole family.

The Children Become More Responsible in the Home

When partnerships end, children might take on the role of the spouse or more responsibilities at home. Dad may no longer be around to pick up a younger sibling after school, so the older sibling might take over this job. Notwithstanding a child's willingness to accommodate the family, the child might resent their parents for this shift in duties.

The Parents Focus on Their Feelings and Neglect to Check In with the Children

Children are feeling something even when they seem OK. Following a breakup, children need parents to check on them. When a child says they are "OK" or "fine," it's an opportunity for the parent to dig deeper. Change is always hard and requires emotional processing, even for kids.

The Family Unit Has Been Changed Forever

Living happily ever after isn't a reality for all partnerships. Both children and parents grieve the loss of the relationship and what life could've been like if it had worked out. Parents shouldn't ignore that a breakup feels like grief to both them and their children.

Repairing the Damage

Forgive Yourself

Pity parenting is the source of many codependent relationships. Parents will make mistakes. So forgive yourself for not knowing better or for not making better choices. Don't just focus on what you didn't do well. Praise yourself for what you did well, and build on your strengths as a parent going forward.

Develop More Empathy

Compassion is the key to becoming a better parent. Parents can develop compassion by considering their children's feelings and understanding themselves, including how they experienced life as a child. Adults are experts on childhood because they all had one. Tap into what it was like to experience life's changes at certain ages, and you will better understand how your children feel.

Understand Your Own Childhood

Stop parenting out of habit. Some things your parents did for you might've been helpful, while others weren't. Don't repeat parenting patterns that weren't helpful or healthy for you. Be open to considering new ways instead of saying things like, "That's how it was for me, and you have to do it, too." Times have changed, and so should your parenting methods.

Embrace Imperfections

Repeat after me: There is no such thing as a perfect parent. Your children will be both pleased and displeased with you no matter how well you parent them. I've found that people who tend to be conscious of their parenting are more likely to do a good job. It's healthy to worry about the impact you have on your children. But turn those worries into actions, intentional conversations with your children, and self-compassion when needed. You won't get everything right, but that's OK.

There is no such thing as a perfect parent.

Acknowledge the Error of Your Ways

It can make a world of difference in a relationship when you acknowledge how you affected the other person. Showing remorse doesn't mean that you're a terrible person, just someone who is continuing to learn and open to exploring how you can improve. When making amends with your child:

- Listen to their perspective without defending your actions or proclaiming your intentions. It's vital that your child feels heard and that their needs are validated.
- Thank them for allowing you space to share and listen. Recognize your child's willingness to speak with you.

- Ask, "What do you need now?" You can't correct anything from the past, but moving forward, find out what your child needs from you. How can the relationship be different?
- Regularly check in about the relationship. Preemptively ask, "How are things going with us?" This is particularly helpful for children who have presented as angry or passive-aggressive.
- Hold space for them to bring up the past. While you don't want past transgressions to be constantly thrown in your face, you can't ignore how they might still be hurtful to your children. So create a safe space for them to discuss their feelings about past issues. By no means should you allow them to use you as a punching bag, however, and they must remain verbally respectful as they bring up situations that hurt them.

Things You Can't Control

You can't manage aspects of your adult child's life, and giving them space to grow up and be their own person is healthy for the relationship. Adult children are, most importantly, *adults*. Even when a parent disagrees with an adult child, sharing that opposition can cause damage to the relationship.

Shifting into a relationship between two adults can be uncomfortable for both parties. The adult children struggle not to offend, while the parent tries to figure out their place. But remember that when your children are young, you're raising future adults. The parent-child relationship tends to shift as children become more autonomous.

The initial shift begins when a child is a teenager, as they begin to spend more time away from parents and with friends. Next, children move out of their parents' home, start serious romantic relationships, and maybe have their own children. In each phase, parents relinquish more control over their children. It's unhealthy for a parent to maintain the same level of control over adult children as when they were younger.

What to Do If You Want a Healthy Relationship with an Adult Child

- **Give them the freedom to make their own choices.** Encourage them to figure things out without you giving them the answer. You want your child to learn to make healthy decisions without your input.
- **Practice asking, "Do you want my opinion?"** If you think it's necessary to step in, ask permission. If they answer yes, let them vent and work through solutions with you.
- **Stop telling them what's best.** You've *raised* them; you're no longer *raising* them.
- **Create new rules of engagement.** Traditions change, desires change, and as a result, how you engage will shift during the relationship. When children first move away from home, contact may be more frequent. As they find their footing, however, twice a day may become once a day and end up becoming once a week or less.
- **Stop holding who they used to be over their head.** Let your children change. Don't guilt-trip them into being the version of themselves that you liked most. "You used to call me every day, but now, you're too busy."
- **Learn to share.** Children will get married and have in-laws, partners, a social life, and careers that will cause shifts in your relationship with them.
- **Make room for boundaries.** Parents aren't entitled to unlimited access to their children.

- **Be the change you wish to see.** *Parent: "My children never call me." Therapist: "Are you calling them?" Parent: "No, they're too busy."* If you want something different to happen, make the first move. Don't put your expectations on others without doing your part.

When you think of a parent's healthy relationship with their adult children, consider how adults treat other adults in their life, including coworkers and friends. Ideally there is mutual respect, understanding, and room for differences in those relationships. Parents' relationships with adult children thrive when adult children are given the same considerations as other adults.

Adult children still need parenting (mothering and fathering). You never outgrow needing someone to nurture you. Some adults are abandoned because their parents have stopped parenting them in adulthood. Parenting is a lifetime commitment. A person can be done raising their children. However, other needs still exist. When you become an adult, your needs look different, but they don't disappear.

Remember: parenting adult children is about supporting them, not managing them.

Common Reasons for Strife

Parents can't pick their kids, and loving them no matter what won't resolve core issues. You can love people and not like them, and you can love people and not want them in your life. Personality, temperament, and life experiences all determine the quality of the parent-child relationship.

Substance misuse, mental health issues, and different lifestyles are common reasons that parents report challenging relationships with their children. Unconditional love doesn't mean that a parent has to tolerate any type of behavior. Essentially, all relationships, even parent-child ones, come with conditions.

Substance Misuse

Substance misuse can cause intolerable and unsafe shifts in a child's personality. Parents may choose to have firm and clear boundaries or manage the relationship from a distance. Parents determine where they draw the line, and for some, no contact may be the healthiest option. In some cases, one parent may choose to handle the child in a way that doesn't make sense to the other parent. When a child has a substance misuse issue, different parenting styles can range from denial to severing ties while the other parent maintains the relationship. It's unfortunate when parents disagree on how to have a relationship with children who misuse substances. Couples therapy could be a space for parents to acknowledge and sort through differences in handling different perspectives about parenting.

Janine and her husband, Ronald, raised their grandchildren. Ronald refused to allow their daughter to see them after she lost custody of them. Janine occasionally spoke to her daughter by phone and allowed her to speak to the children.

Religion

Converting or adopting a new religion can strain the relationship between parent and child. Religion impacts how you view the world, and in some cases, those views may cause a child to change the way they engage with family. When family members argue over doctrines, history, and religious facts, then tensions or ruptures can ensue in some cases. Parents can be most comfortable with a child choosing to stay as the parents taught them. A considerable part of adulthood is deciding who you want to be.

When Your Child Chooses a Different Religious Path, You Can
- Respect your child's preference to explore a new faith
- Become curious about the new religion by seeking to learn more on your own and listen to what your child shares
- Participate in activities around the new religion
- Avoid heated conversations about religion that will lead to an argument
- Highlight the positive impacts of religion on your child's life
- Unite around topics that have nothing to do with religion

LGBTQIA+

Many have come a long way with acceptance, yet many families have a significant way to go. One of the biggest fears I've heard from parents of LGBTQIA+ parents is their fear for their child's safety. Due to this fear, parents have encouraged children to hide who they are. This is damaging to the child's self-esteem. And it is hard to keep a significant part of who you are secret.

Parents feel shame and sometimes blame themselves. Emery's father, Larry, had always called her "tomboyish." When she told him she was interested in girls, Larry said it was just a phase. Immediately, Larry started making a big deal about how she dressed and what type of girls she was hanging around. Emery knew who she was, but her father refused to accept it.

For Parents
- It is helpful to find a therapist to help you process what your expectations were for your child.
- Be respectful of who your child is even if it's not what you desire for them. Remember, it's not easy to accept who you are, and being rejected makes it harder.

- Educate yourself on how your child would like to be addressed.
- Your child may become someone different from what you planned. Pity won't change things, and it can make things worse.

Remember This: To have a better relationship with your child, you will need to learn to accept who they are.

For Children
- Allow time for your parents to adjust to becoming more aware of who you are.
- Set boundaries around your pronouns and expectations for how you want to be treated.
- Seek therapy as a way to process the changes in your relationship with your parents.
- If the relationship becomes unhealthy in ways that impact your mental health, determine if you want to remain in the relationship, leave, or take space.

Mental Health Issues

It's painful for most parents when their child declines treatment for mental health issues. My former neighbor had a son who was diagnosed with schizophrenia. She warned me about opening my door for him if he happened to stop by. After years of trying to coax him into staying on medication and attending therapy, she chose to stop fighting him. Because of previous incidents of violence, he was no longer allowed in her home. This was a hard choice for her, but a necessary one.

Lifestyle Differences

Adult children decide who they become when they grow up. They may even choose to not be the type of person you raised them to be.

Lifestyle differences might include

Financial choices
Traditional vs. nontraditional romantic relationships
Diets
Political views

Eva has had a contentious relationship with her son, Miles, since he married Amber five years ago. Amber has been controlling and seems to create distance between Miles and everyone he loves. To Eva, it's as if her Miles is no longer the sweet person she raised, as he allows Amber to ruin his relationships with everyone else.

The desire to repair a parent-child relationship is sometimes on only one side, but repair can't take place unless and until both sides want it.

Raising Adults

Sometimes, adult children don't launch as planned, but that doesn't mean it's helpful to continue treating them like kids. It's understandable for a parent to worry and do all they can to help adult children care for themselves, but doing so can cost parents dearly. A study from MagnifyMoney found that 22 percent of adults of all ages, but 67 percent of Generation Z, receive financial support from their parents. When the adult child would probably fail without support, some parents unintentionally create a codependent relationship.

In a study by Bankrate, 34 percent of parents put their retirement funds at risk by taking care of their adult children's housing, health insurance, or emergency expenses. The solution is complicated and may require help from professionals, such as financial advisers or therapists. But the solution shouldn't solely depend on the parents.

Parents want to ensure that children are cared for at any age, and it's important to remember to help without enabling adult children.

Helping an adult child might look like:

- Offering support on a temporary, limited-time basis
- Teaching a child how to do something instead of doing it for them
- Placing boundaries on how you're able to support them
- Allowing them to find solutions without giving them the answers or taking care of the problem
- Slowly moving away from the role of caregiver to a more supportive role

When an adult child functions without boundaries, parents must figure out how to parent differently for the long-term benefits of the child. Support must be offered with boundaries and not to the detriment of the parents.

Solutions to Relationship Challenges with Adult Children

Family Therapy

Therapy is a space for all parties to be supported. Taking care of problems on our own isn't always the best solution. Family issues may require the help of a skilled professional. In therapy, issues surface that would never have been addressed otherwise.

If you are the person interested in family therapy, it might be helpful to invite your loved one to join you in one of these ways:

> "I love you, and I want to work on our relationship. I've found a family therapist. Would you like to go to therapy with me?"

"I realize that when we attempt to talk through things on our
own, it often ends in an argument. I would love for us to talk
to a professional about the way we communicate."

"This relationship is important to me; please come to therapy
with me."

Individual Therapy

When a family member won't go to therapy or you aren't ready to invite
them to join you, go on your own to work through the issues as best you
can. It's common for people in therapy to discuss their relationships with
people who aren't in therapy with them. You can learn to manage a difficult relationship and process your feelings without the other person present. Individual therapy is a place for you to work on yourself and how you
function in your relationships with others.

Parenting Younger Children: You Can Shape the Future

You can change your future by doing things differently and refusing to
repeat unhealthy cycles with your children. What problems exist in your
family, and what do you need to do to create a different outcome for yourself? Let's talk about a few ways to break generational patterns.

Encourage Your Kids to Talk About Their Feelings

When Sidney was eleven years old, her parents divorced. She and her siblings learned about it only when their father packed and left the house. No
one told them what was happening. They were just told, "Everything will
be OK." But the kids didn't feel OK, because their lives were changing in a
significant way.

Whenever Sidney attempted to talk about the divorce, her mother changed the subject. Sidney eventually stopped talking about anything that bothered her, but this was harmful because children need an emotional connection with the adults in their lives.

Feelings are often a taboo and ignored topic in families. Nevertheless, feelings exist even when we aren't talking about them. Even when there's a crisis in the family, kids are aware of it, and it helps them feel less alone to talk about their feelings with adults.

Be careful not to overdeliver on the promise that "everything will be OK" or "it isn't that bad." Sometimes, it *won't* be OK, and it *is* that bad. As an adult, you can listen to how your children feel. You might not be able to do anything about the situation, but talking about complicated feelings shows that you're connected to them and care about helping them through it.

Teaching children to be emotionally detached looks like:

- Shaming them for being sensitive
- Stopping them from showing emotions
- Pushing them to get over their feelings before they're ready
- Saying things like "You're OK" when they're upset
- Telling them how to feel
- Forcing them to agree with you about how they "should" feel
- Avoiding conversations about feelings
- Not allowing them to see you express emotions
- Appearing as if you always have it together

Apologize to Children When You're Wrong

I've learned from being a parent that I don't know everything. I get things wrong, and when I mess up, I should apologize. When I was a child, I saw some adults making excuses and doubling down when they were wrong. They didn't apologize or admit that what they said or did was inaccurate. It's courageous to admit ignorance over faking wisdom.

It's helpful to apologize to kids when:

- You yelled out of anger or frustration
- You emotionally neglected or dismissed them
- You were wrong
- You placed them in a situation to take care of themselves without proper guidance from an adult
- You blamed them for something inaccurately
- You mistreated them

Apologies don't always make things better, but they let your child know you're willing to be accountable for your part in the situation.

Apologizing to a child might sound like:

- "I yelled, and it wasn't appropriate. I apologize."
- "You were trying to talk to me earlier and I wasn't listening. I'm sorry. Can you repeat now what you were saying?"
- "I misunderstood the facts. You were right."
- "You weren't supposed to know how to do that without support. I should've been around to help you."
- "I'm sorry I blamed you. It was my fault."
- "Please forgive me for speaking to you that way. It wasn't appropriate."

Allow Your Kids to See You Being Emotional, and Explain Your Feelings to Them

Covering up your pain isn't healthy for you or your children. It takes strength to be vulnerable enough to share your emotions with others. Too often, I've heard clients say, "I've never seen my mother get upset. She's always calm." Normalizing your feelings can help children feel comfortable expressing theirs. In an age-appropriate manner, share what you're feeling.

Sharing your feelings might sound like this:

- "I'm crying because my mother died, and I miss her."
- "I yelled because I was upset."
- "I'm going to take a few minutes to myself because I'm frustrated."

Don't deny your feelings to kids when they see you experiencing something difficult. If so, they won't know how to respond organically when something similar happens to them. Kids can handle your honesty. You don't have to pretend by saying "I'm not upset" or "I'm OK."

Of course, there are times when adults share too many details or share too often, but sharing occasionally isn't too much as long as you don't turn your children into your emotional caretakers. If you find that you're talking about your feelings too much with your children, it might be a sign that you need another adult to talk to, such as a mental health professional.

Spend Time with Your Kids Doing What They Want

According to a recent study, quality time is more impactful than quantity. Luckily, today parents tend to be more willing to play, read to their children, and engage in child-related activities.

There's no exact number as to what constitutes "enough" quality time, but doing things that matter to your children is crucial. They want to know that you care about what's important to them, which is why they make bids for your attention by saying, "Look at my drawing," or "Watch TV with me."

Adults from dysfunctional families often didn't have parents who stepped into their world, and when they did, they were too rigid to engage in fun. Instead, they might have pushed their child to participate in sports, but that isn't the same as engaging in the child's world. The child must be interested, not simply forced or even willing to participate in an activity. The parent must be directly involved in that activity by helping the child practice or by attending games. Rather than choose an activity for your child, ask them what *they* would like to do.

Teach Them Healthy Ways to Deal with Triggers

We all get emotionally triggered in big and small ways. Children have tantrums because they're emotionally dysregulated. So it's beneficial to teach them a few strategies to self-regulate (by themselves) or co-regulate (with others).

Self-regulation can look like:

- Independent deep breathing
- Playing with a fidget toy
- Journaling

Co-regulation can look like:

- Talking about their concerns
- Deep breathing with others
- Hugging

Be the Person They Need and the Person You Wish You Had

You're a child expert because you used to be a child. Recall what it was like to feel out of control. Remember how it felt to have to rely on adults for most things. Tap into what you needed, revisiting your childhood self to understand better how to nurture your children.

Humans are unique; each of us needs something a little different. Because we all need different things, it's impossible to parent two children the same and meet their unique needs. Also, parenting your children from the perspective of "this is what I needed" won't be effective. Children need you to be what they uniquely need while also remembering what it was like to be a child.

Over time, the level of parenting required shifts from a more hands-on approach to one where you're supporting the lifestyle that your child wants for themselves. Shifts in the parent-child relationship can be complicated, yet they're healthy as the child grows and develops. With each step of a child's growth, a parent relinquishes a little more control. It can be hard for children to transition into the adult-child role. This is done well when parents support their children in becoming adults, remembering that love isn't defined by control.

EXERCISE

Grab your journal or a piece of paper to complete the following prompts:

* What are/were your hopes for the parent-child relationship?
* What do your children need to hear from you?
* What boundaries do you need to support your child?

CHAPTER 14

Troubleshooting Relationships with Extended Family

Families often struggle to manage their expectations around loss, and relationships can be tested. The death of Avery's grandfather Albert left her family in a state of disruption when certain aunts, uncles, and cousins were left out of his will. The ones who received an inheritance were expected to give a portion of their share to those who were omitted. It was a mess.

Albert seemed to love all five of his children, but over the years, it became clear that his eldest son and daughter were his favorites. While living, he provided financial gifts to all five adult children to some extent, but in the will, he left funds and possessions only to the two oldest children and two of his twelve grandchildren.

After Albert's death, the family no longer gathered for holidays because everyone argued about the will. Avery's father, who was the middle child, stopped communicating with his two younger sisters.

Avery had never really connected with her grandfather, so she wasn't surprised when she wasn't named in the will. She couldn't understand why her father and aunts wouldn't put their differences aside for the sake of the family. She saw it as her grandfather's choice, but she knew that sharing her opinion honestly could turn her into an outcast in the family.

She had grown up spending a lot of time with her cousins, aunts, and uncles. But now that everyone was at odds, she found it increasingly difficult to maintain those connections. She didn't want to take sides, yet she didn't want to sneak around to talk to her relatives. Whenever she did talk to her aunts, they gossiped about their older siblings.

Avery was engaged to be married and wanted to invite her extended family to the wedding, but she worried about having them all in the same room. She tried to work through seating options to ensure that everyone would remain separate, but she knew her father would be upset with her for inviting them.

Avery wanted to tell her father that she would invite his brother and all his sisters to the wedding. She sought therapy to deal with his anger about what he might consider a betrayal.

Caught in the Middle

Even family issues that have nothing to do with you can affect you. If your parents are at odds with their siblings, it can get in the way of your relationships with your aunts, uncles, cousins, and grandparents. But you can't force anyone to repair relationships.

Avery wanted to remain neutral, which had worked out fine as long as she didn't call on others to engage with one another. She had been able to secretly visit and communicate with her aunt and uncle on their turf, but her wedding was complicating matters.

What Might Help Avery
Being honest

Even though it might upset some, Avery can be honest about wanting to maintain relationships with everyone despite their personal issues with each other.

Setting boundaries

Avery can let everyone know that she won't be a container for their issues. That might sound like this:

> *To her father:* "Dad, I understand you're upset about being left out of the will. Aside from your issues with your siblings, I don't have any, and I want to see them from my point of view."

> *To her aunts, uncle, and cousins:* "I want our relationship to be based on us, not the issues you have with the other people I love."

Allowing people to choose

When Avery hosts events, some people might choose not to come in order to avoid other attendees. She can't control if they show up and will need to learn how to deal with the discomfort of everyone not getting along.

Staying neutral

It isn't your job to manage family disputes or act as the family therapist. Perhaps your job is to let others know that you'll be a neutral party, and you don't want to be a part of the drama.

Family rifts often start as a result of inheritance issues, harmful gossip, patterns of chronic dysfunction such as addiction or abuse, or favoritism among family members. If you watch any family dramas, such as *Parenthood*, *This Is Us*, or *Succession*, one of the above dynamics is always at play. On the series *Shameless*, for example, each family member is uniquely dysfunctional. Even so, the patriarch, Frank Gallagher, has a favorite son, Liam, perhaps because he's the youngest and has the most positive view of Frank's dysfunction. Liam doesn't yet have as much of a history with

Frank as his five siblings do. Therefore, his image of his dad isn't as distorted. Also, Frank pays attention to the relationship, possibly because this is his last opportunity to get fatherhood right.

Common Issues with Grandparents, Aunts, Uncles, and Cousins

Arguing About Old Issues

History repeats itself in many families, sometimes for generations—until someone is brave enough to talk about the family's problems. Talking is different from arguing, however, which involves yelling and never getting your point across. Of course, some family issues run so deep that a professional may be needed, or you may have to just let them go.

At family gatherings, Sally's mother, aunts, and uncles always argued about things that happened in their childhood. At first, it would start as a lighthearted conversation, but it would inevitably escalate into shouting. Sally began to avoid family gatherings because she couldn't stand the heated disputes among the elders.

Ways to manage this issue:

- Understand that not all issues can be resolved, and commit to stop bringing them up.
- Let problems go when your peace of mind is at stake.
- Talk about issues one-on-one instead of in large groups.
- Leave early before arguments get heated.

Feeling Left Out

You might have heard the saying "If you want to find out who someone is, wait for a birth, a wedding, or a death." Families experience their greatest challenges during significant life events, so it's important to talk about expectations beforehand.

For example, Miguel was close with his aunt, Patrice. For his wedding to his partner, she assumed that since she was his favorite, she'd be more involved with the planning. While he was busy putting the event together, Miguel spoke less and less with his aunt, and she became upset about being left out.

It makes sense that we have expectations about our relationships with others. However, we cannot control whether people will meet those expectations. As we mature and meet new people, our desires for our relationships shift. As you are introduced to other relationships or your desires change, some family members may feel left out. It's possible that your sister isn't your maid of honor or that your once-favorite cousin isn't invited to your house gathering. You change, and that changes your relationships.

Ways to manage this issue:

- Speak up early. "The two of us want to plan the wedding as a way of learning to work together."
- Make sure the other person hears you. "I want to make sure that you understand what I said. What did you hear me say?"

Hurtful Comments

Most families have at least one rude or mean relative. Many family members will say, "That's just the way they are." Fortunately, you don't have to tolerate people who are mean even when others accept the behavior.

Hearing "Remember the time you peed in my bed?" over Thanksgiving dinner might start to sting after a while. Families may see teasing as a connective behavior. At some point, the jokes might start to move from funny to hurtful, and you should let your family know when the jokes aren't acceptable anymore. "It was just a joke" is gaslighting, not a joke.

Making harsh statements and pretending that those statements are jokes is gaslighting. Gaslighting is hurtful because the other person is essentially saying, "Rather than admit the truth, I will make you believe you're out of your mind." Because it's so shocking that someone would do this, you wreck your brain trying to figure out if you have lost your mind. The truth is, it's not you, and you are *not* out of your mind. Gaslighting is an abusive tool used to make you question yourself.

When Chris gained weight, multiple family members brought it up at family gatherings, and some even made jokes about it. Chris was hurt but didn't know how to get them to stop.

Ways to manage this issue:

- Speak up. "Stop talking about my weight. It's not funny; it's mean."
- Repeat yourself. "I mentioned this before. I'm aware that I've gained weight. It isn't helpful for you to repeat the obvious."
- Consider how frequently or infrequently you want to engage with your family when your requests have been repeatedly ignored.

Being Different from Everyone Else

We are always growing and changing—sometimes in a direction that strays from the family norm. This can be hard for family members to accept. It isn't that they don't want you to do well, but seeing someone change can be a reminder that they haven't.

Tamara divorced her husband after two years of marriage and one child. She was ostracized by her family, who believed heavily in marriage. If there was an issue in your marriage, divorce wasn't an option.

Missy was the only one of her cousins to complete college. Once she became an attorney, her family teased her about being "bougie." When she answered their questions, they gathered information to later throw in her face. Missy felt like she had to withhold who she was from her family.

Ways to manage this issue:

- Be yourself. Pretending to be someone you aren't is damaging to your mental health.
- Know that you can't change your family's perception. They see you based on their own limitations, not yours. You can't control their desire to want you to stay the same.
- Find common ground as best you can.

Ways to create the life you want:

- Put yourself out into the world despite what your family might say.
- Be kind to your family without enabling them.
- Build new habits.
- Accept that some people won't agree with every decision you make for yourself.
- Believe in yourself even when others don't.

Debates

Political views, COVID-19 vaccinations, racial injustice, open relationships, sexual identity, and more can be challenging topics for families to discuss. Instead of understanding, many family members will argue to try to change each other's minds or reject someone's belief system or lifestyle. The trick is to keep living and stop trying to change the people who refuse to understand you.

One day, Megan decided she no longer wanted to hide. So she brought her partner home for Thanksgiving, even though she knew her family wasn't supportive of her same-sex relationship. She was getting older, and their opinion no longer mattered as much. Even though her grandparents had something to say, her parents and siblings accepted her for who she truly is.

Ways to manage this issue:

- Recognize that your family doesn't have to agree with your decisions.
- Have conversations with individuals beforehand about what you expect from their behavior. They should grant you respect even if they don't agree with or accept your choices.
- Consider removing yourself from situations where you feel demeaned or ridiculed for being who you are. You can't change other people, and you don't have to be present with them.
- Refuse to fight. An argument is between two people, so you can decline to argue with anyone if you wish.

Inheritance Issues

Family relationships can get especially tricky when money is involved. Some members may feel entitled to an inheritance based on their relationship with the deceased person. Families may fight when they believe others didn't deserve to receive the money. When inheritances come as a surprise and people feel left out, a battle can break out among the living.

Avery's situation after her grandfather's death was unfair, but she could choose how she wanted to respond to the resulting family discord.

Ways to manage this issue:

- Ask a question instead of assuming you know someone's motives.
- Know who you're angry with, and don't take that anger out on others. You can't control how another person chooses to spend their money or to whom they decide to leave their assets.
- If you feel comfortable, be open about your financial plans after your death so that there are no surprises among your heirs.

Remember This: Relatives are the people you're related to by blood, and family consists of the people who offer you a sense of belonging, acceptance, and connection. If you want to maintain relationships, you might have to accept that some family members won't fit your ideal image. You may have to meet them where they are and resist the urge to pull them up to your level. Some issues are worth fighting for, while others are not. You don't have to tolerate mistreatment from people just because you're related to them.

EXERCISE

Grab your journal or a piece of paper to complete the following prompts:

* What are some of the key issues in your extended family relationships?
* Who do you feel the most distant from in your family, and who do you feel closest to?
* What barriers have you faced in attempting to improve relationships with your extended family?

CHAPTER 15

Navigating In-Laws

Many of my clients complain about in-laws. Nia dreamed of having an excellent relationship with her mother-in-law, Doris. After all, her own mother wasn't what she'd hoped for, so she relished the chance for a do-over on a close mother-daughter relationship.

Unfortunately, Doris failed to meet Nia's expectations. Instead of her dream coming true, Nia became trapped in a nightmare. Doris was controlling and mean, and acted more like her son's girlfriend than his parent. Still, Nia seemed to be the only one who had a problem with Doris's overbearing nature.

At first, they got along well. But when Nia and her husband, Will, were buying their first home, the problems began. Will didn't talk to Nia first about housing options; he spoke to his mother. Doris's offer to assist with a down payment came with opinions ranging from location to decor. She felt free to give unsolicited advice and even meddle in Nia's relationship with her son from a previous relationship and her own mother.

This led to fights between Nia and Will, who always seemed to see things from his mother's point of view. Because Nia didn't have a healthy relationship with her own mother, Will told her that what she saw as overbearing was healthy and normal. Frustrated, disappointed, and angry, Nia questioned her sanity. Was she being irrational, biased, and unkind?

Since she was unsure about what was appropriate, she sought therapy. "I'm tired of fighting about someone who doesn't live in our house," she told me. "I love my husband, but I can't live like this. We'll get along for a second, but then Doris will be back to her antics of trying to run our lives. I try to let my husband handle it, but he doesn't."

Family by Marriage

Many people feel obligated to have a relationship with their in-laws even when the situation isn't healthy. In fact, your partner has a particular relationship with their family, and you can choose what type of relationship to have with your in-laws. You are not obligated to endure unhealthy relationships with people, including your in-laws—nor can you mold them into the ideal versions of themselves that you've imagined. When you stop expecting a mother-in-law to be your ideal mother figure, you can accept them as they are and create a cordial or close relationship. When you stop expecting your sister-in-law to be less this or more that, you can accept her for who she is and develop the best relationship for each party or decide the relationship isn't substantiable.

A cordial relationship might look like:

Greeting them
Speaking to your in-law as needed
Minimizing conversations that might lead to arguing
Deciding how much time you will spend at a family gathering

Deciding if you want to be at family gatherings

Considering whether they should stay in your home while
    visiting, or if you'll stay in theirs

I am not condoning acting passive-aggressively toward your in-laws by doing things such as intentionally leaving them out. However, I suggest that you choose your engagement level in the relationship. In-laws are not the family you choose; they are the family you marry into. You determine what your relationship looks like with your in-laws. Sometimes the kindest thing you can do for someone is allow distance between you and them. Choose to be cordial, not close.

Choose to be cordial, not close.

Strive for Acceptance

The term "in-laws" includes anyone from your partner's family of origin. Some people enter these relationships with the expectation of having a second set of parents or best sister-in-law. Tempering your expectations can save you potential disappointment. This doesn't mean you should have no expectations. Just be realistic. It might be hard to accept that your in-laws can't fulfill your deep desires, but accepting them as they are will be more helpful than trying to change them into your ideal people.

Issue: Your sister-in-law gossips to you about other members of
    the family.

Acceptance: Only share things you don't mind sharing with
    other people.

Be cautious about sharing your feelings with people who

- Tell you how to feel
- Dismiss your feelings
- Can't be happy for you
- Try to get you to move on without processing your feelings
- Seem too distracted to listen
- Appear consumed with their own issues
- Immediately tell you what you did "wrong"
- Press you to share beyond your comfort level
- Quickly judge your character

Issue: Your father-in-law doesn't have a relationship with his grandchildren.

Acceptance:
- Don't make excuses for his absence.
- Forge relationships with other people who are healthy supports for your children.
- Remember that supporters don't have to be family members.

There are exceptions to every rule, but people are usually who they've shown themselves to be in the past. Stop acting surprised when they behave as they always have.

You Are Stepping into a Preexisting Family

As an outsider, you will likely see things differently from others. Entering relationships with the mission to change them will do more harm than good. Seek to understand the relationship dynamics instead of trying to change them immediately. The dynamics you see unfolding are sometimes not an issue for your in-laws.

Nia saw her mother-in-law as overbearing; Will saw the same behavior as loving. Perhaps it would be helpful for Nia to state what she wants instead of trying to get her husband to see the issue from her point of view.

> *Example: Doris wants to help with a down payment and begins sharing her suggestions as to where they should live.*
> Possible solution: Nia and Will make a list to determine what they want in their future home. When Will brings up his mother's suggestions, Nia refers him back to their list instead of talking about her mother-in-law's feedback.

> *Example: Doris wants her grandson to stay overnight, which Nia feels is too soon for him at his age.*
> Possible solution: Nia shares her concerns with Will and discusses when it's appropriate to try an overnight visit.

In my work with clients, they report the following challenges with in-laws:

- Communicating with a partner's ex
- Judgment and criticism
- Not respecting your time
- Parenting differences
- Doing things they were asked not to do with your children
- Overinvolvement in marital disputes
- Guilt-tripping about family involvement

- Religious differences
- Not respecting privacy
- Gossiping with other family members
- Making big couple moments about them
- Codependent and enmeshed relationships
- Stealing the show
- Constantly offering unsolicited advice
- Helpful, but with strings attached or a desire to control the situation

This list is not exhaustive, but it does cover quite a few common challenges in in-law relationships.

What to Do About Common Challenges

Communicating with a Partner's Ex

In-laws may get attached to your partner's ex even though you find it offensive. They may maintain relationships with an ex who seemed like "part of the family." When possible, have your partner address this behavior with their family. When your partner won't, you may need to have an uncomfortable conversation with your in-laws.

This might be helpful:

- Let them know that conversations about the ex make you feel uncomfortable.
- Set expectations in your relationship about how you want your partner to handle interactions with their ex.
- You can't control your in-laws' relationships with other people, but you can let them know how having those relationships makes you feel.

Remember that some exes have become family when children are involved. In these situations, it is helpful to maintain healthy contact. Sometimes, in-laws can act as buffers when exes who are co-parents are feuding.

Judgment and Criticism

Judgments become problematic when someone verbally announces their opinions to others. Nia's mother-in-law, Doris, shamed her for not having a healthier relationship with her own mother, saying over and over again, "You only get one mother." That belief may have worked for Doris, but not for Nia.

This might be helpful:

- Accept that your in-laws might have a different idea of what family relationships should look like, and you don't have to try to fit their standards.
- Name instances when your in-law is being judgmental. "Despite my mother being mean to me, you tell me I'm terrible for not wanting a relationship with her—you're being critical."
- Share only what they need to know, not things they will judge or criticize.

Not Respecting Your Time

Your time doesn't belong to your in-laws. If you want them to be considerate of your time, you will likely have to change the way you allow them to use it.

In-laws: "We're going to the beach in July, and we'll pay for everything."

You have the option to say no.

In-laws: "This is my granddaughter's first Christmas, and we
    can't wait to spoil her rotten."
        You have the option to set limits on gift-giving for your
    child.

In-laws: "We'd like you to stay over on Christmas Eve."
        You have the option to plan your own holiday.

This might be helpful:

- Share your holiday plans early.
- Agree to things when it works best for you and the people involved
  in your holiday plans.
- Before agreeing to anything, talk to your partner.

Parenting Differences

Your parenting style may seem offensive to in-laws because it might hold
up a mirror to how they parented. When an in-law mentions the differences or makes a suggestion, advocate for your approach.

Advocating for your parenting style might sound like this:

- "I hear that you didn't do things this way. This is my preference,
  and I'd like you to respect it."
- "When you correct me in front of my children, it undermines my
  authority."
- "Thank you for your suggestion. We're doing things differently."
- "This is what's been recommended by our doctor and is in line
  with the current medical research."

People can make suggestions, but if the information doesn't apply to you, disregard it. And if in-laws constantly make unhealthy suggestions, ask them to stop.

Saying "stop" might sound like:

- "It's hard for me to process all these suggestions. I need to listen to my voice. Please stop telling me what to do."
- "I know you've been parenting longer, so when I need something, I will ask."
- "When I'm ready for feedback, I will ask you directly."

Your in-laws don't have to agree with your parenting style, and there will likely be some differences. Use your voice to speak up for your family's needs. In the meantime, it's OK to be upset about their comments or concerned about what they think. However, don't start believing that you need to abandon a parenting style that works for you and your family.

Doing Things They Were Asked Not to Do with Your Children

Even when you're vocal about your expectations, in-laws might have other ideas. I once overheard an in-law say, "It didn't make sense for a child who had a nut allergy to have to always go without peanuts." Parents must be on guard and present in cases where in-laws don't respect major safety issues.

Some situations aren't debatable, while others are. With your partner, it's helpful to decide if you'll accept your kids having more sugar while with Grandma or if sugar poses an issue for the child, even if it's only once in a while. For your children and household, the rules are created by you and your partner. People may not like respecting them, but your rules don't have to be debatable.

This might be helpful:

- State your issue in real time or soon after. "Please don't give them any more of that," or "The other day when you were here, I asked you not to____, and in the future I would like____."
- Affirm the difference in how you parent and how they might want to direct your children.
- Remind them that you are acting in your child's best interest and doing what works best for your family.
- Let them know that you want them to have a relationship with your children, and to do so it's important that they honor your requests.

Overinvolvement in Marital Disputes

Sometimes, partners will use their family as a sounding board. As a result, in-laws may stick their noses too far into your business.

How to Handle In-Laws Offering Unsolicited Advice
- Attempt to get on the same page as your partner, if possible.
- Verbally say, "I don't want you weighing in on our relationship."
- When your in-laws attempt to get involved, remind them their involvement isn't wanted.
- Encourage your partner to go to couples therapy if they need a sounding board.

In-laws sometimes carry grudges long after disputes are settled between partners. Inviting biased parties into a relationship can damage the couple, as well as the relationship with the in-laws. Fight your own battles.

Fight your own battles.

Guilt-Tripping About Family Involvement

A nuclear family consists of those in your home and your dependents. Prioritizing the needs of an extended family can negatively impact your nuclear family.

Every summer, Rachel planned the family beach trip, which included about twenty relatives. Planning was stressful, and when stressed, she became more irritable with her partner and their two children. At first, getting people to commit to dates, location, and activities seemed fun. Then, it became a job she no longer wanted. Whenever she mentioned pulling back and letting someone else handle the planning, her mother-in-law would remind her how good she was at planning and how everyone depended on her.

People may guilt-trip you, but you don't have to feel guilty for choosing your sanity.

When people attempt to guilt-trip you, practice saying things like:

- "It sounds like you didn't like my answer, but I'm not going to change it."
- "We can want different things."
- "You're trying to make me feel bad."
- "I'm not shifting my boundary."
- "You're pushing against my limits."
- "Stop trying to make me feel bad for wanting something different from you."
- "I expressed my position, and I'm not changing my mind."
- "I hear what you're saying, and my answer is still no."

Religious Differences

Religion impacts culture, and culture impacts family dynamics. It would be too simplistic to say, "Just don't talk about it." Even within the same religion, there are different denominations. When we care about a cause, it's natural to want others to feel the same. Therefore, you may want some-one to have the same religious views.

When your in-laws are insistent on having your child baptized when it's not what you want, or trying to make you attend certain religious ser-vices, it's OK to kindly ask them to stop and affirm that you've made your choice, which means your children won't be involved either. Perhaps their intention is to motivate you to change your mind. Let them know you're firmly planted in your decision.

To peacefully coexist, try this:

- Focus on what you have in common, not the topics you're divided on.
- Be clear about what's respectful and what's disrespectful.
- If you don't want to talk about religion, refrain from having con-versations about it. Tell others directly that you choose to abstain from heated religious debates.
- Let people know you want the relationship to work despite the differences.

Not Respecting Privacy

Share when you're ready and not one moment before. There are no rules stat-ing that family has to hear everything first. Sometimes, you want to process on your own, with your partner, or with the people in your household.

For example, Denise was three months pregnant when she told her sister-in-law she was expecting again. Her sister-in-law said, "Why did you wait so long to tell us?" This was Denise's third pregnancy after two mis-carriages. She hated telling people when she lost the babies because not only did she have to process her own sadness, but also she had to deal with the questions and sadness of others. It was too much, and she knew with this pregnancy that she couldn't put herself through that again.

Others may have an issue with when or if you choose to share something with them, and you can't control their response. You can choose to withhold your business for any reason. You can share as much or as little as you want. Sometimes you may seek to keep things to yourself because you don't want to be pitied or deal with the other person's response, because you aren't ready to share, or because it's none of their business. Being private is not the same as keeping secrets.

Gossiping with Other Family Members

Sharing private information or fictitious, mean-spirited, or judgmental comments about another person's life is gossip. Gossiping is a common way that people connect with others, and the information is shared without permission and in a way that could harm relationships. In some families, gossiping is a regular, not necessarily healthy, part of a conversational connection. Sometimes, people gossip to express concern. Gossip steers the conversation from the people present to others.

When you are the subject of gossip, it shows a lack of trust in the relationship. You can't stop people from gossiping, but you can control what you share with others. If a family member demonstrates that they cannot keep your secrets private, stop sharing information you don't want to be told to others. If family members are making up information about you, perhaps going to the person who dispensed misinformation with the correct information could help. However, some people will spread a salacious lie because it's more exciting than the truth, or because they are trying to shape a narrative about you.

Be vulnerable and let people know how it makes you feel to be gossiped about:

> "I want to trust you, and it's hard to trust you when you share
> what I say to you with others."

"Stop sharing my business, or I will stop telling you things."
"I'm hurt to know you said mean things about me behind
    my back."

When You Don't Want to Participate in Gossiping, Practice Saying:
- "I don't feel comfortable having this discussion without them present."
- "If they wanted me to know, they would've shared it with me."
- "It's not my business."
- "I'd like to hear more about what's happening with you."
- "I don't have anything to contribute to the conversation."
- "I don't want to be involved."
- "I don't feel comfortable talking about this."

Making Big Couple Moments About Them

Some people can't help but make things about them. Remember that people will be themselves even during your big moments when you notice them hijacking an experience, be it your wedding or your child's birth, or make other big moments about them—remember, this is who they are. Because you accept this doesn't mean you have to tolerate it. Remind them that this experience is about you and your partner or set clear expectations before the event and remind them of the expectation if they violate the boundary.

Acceptance involves not expecting people to be different because it's what you want. They have to be aware of your expectations; and even when they are, some people cannot meet them. If you accept people for who they are without trying to change them, will there be certain parts of your life they won't be able to participate in, or can they partake in a modified way?

Codependent and Enmeshed Relationships

Codependency can be a part of the family culture, and trying to make quick changes in other people's relationships won't work. You can tell your partner the challenges that impact you or your household, but telling them they need to change because it's not your relationship preference might cause more harm than good. Telling your partner how to operate in their relationships seems helpful, but if the dynamics are not bothersome to your partner and the other person, watch and intervene when needed.

Your standards for your relationships can be different from your partner's. It's essential to speak directly to the impact, not necessarily the label of codependency.

> "When you loan your brother money before we pay our bills, it leaves us paying our bills late."
> "Your mother likes to visit without checking first, which infringes on our time together."

Stealing the Show

When Tina married Amari, she took her mother-in-law and mother to pick out dresses. Tina's mother found a beautiful purple dress that coordinated with the bridesmaids' dresses, while Amari's mother insisted on wearing a knee-length white dress. Tina believed only the bride should wear white, and Amari's mother emphasized that she wanted to stand out as the groom's mother.

I've heard far too many stories of mothers-in-law hijacking the wedding or in-laws stealing the show from couples during big moments. In these scenarios, it's helpful to stop pretending that people will be different just because the occasion has changed. Start having conversations about your expectations early, and hold people accountable in the moment.

Examples:

- "My baby shower is coming up, and I know you don't like some of my friends. Please be cordial for my big day."
- "It's my award show, and I know you're excited, but don't yell during my speech."

Constantly Offering Unsolicited Advice

Everyone has an opinion, and when you don't want someone to share their opinion with you, let them know. It might be the unspoken norm in your partner's family for people to voice their opinions.

When family members offer unsolicited advice, practice saying things like this:

- "That's good to know, and I already have a solution."
- "That might work for you, but that's not something I'm comfortable doing."
- "Please stop telling me what I should do."
- "You seem like you're trying to help, and listening would be helpful right now."
- "I want to work through this without input from others."
- "I know you mean well, and it's hard for me to say this, but I don't want any advice, and when I do, I will ask."
- "I'm venting, not looking for advice."

Helpful, but with Strings Attached or a Desire to Control the Situation

Help that comes with control isn't healthy. If in-laws have a history of helping and making demands afterward, be aware of this before accepting their help.

When help comes with strings, try this:

- Seek other sources for support.
- Make them aware of the pattern, and ask them not to make demands.
- Ask them to clearly outline contingencies, and decide if you want to accept the help.
- Stop asking for help.

Relationships with in-laws are challenging because instead of accepting people as they are, we often try to change them into who we'd like them to be. Perhaps your in-laws aren't what you imagined.

Remember This: You can change how you engage with your in-laws and reframe their behaviors.

EXERCISE

Grab your journal or a piece of paper to complete the following prompts:

- ✳ What are the most challenging aspects of your relationships with your in-laws?
- ✳ What behaviors can you change to have better outcomes in these relationships?

CHAPTER 16

Managing Blended Families

Jason loved Tanesha, but her son, Caleb, was such a handful that he questioned why he married her. The couple had three children in total, including Tanesha's two from a previous relationship. Caleb was fourteen years old, Callie was twelve, and Jaden, the child they had together, was three. Callie was respectful and stayed out of the way, while Caleb was sometimes combative and rude.

Jason and Tanesha had different parenting styles, but since Jason was a new parent, Tanesha didn't accept his feedback. He often said, "I'm a man, and I know that boys don't need to be spoiled by their mothers." Tanesha disagreed and parented the way she always had.

The couple only fought about parenting, and Jason didn't want his young son to be raised like Tanesha's other children.

Because of Caleb's behavior, Jason often excluded his stepchildren in family gatherings with his side of the family. Plus, when they were all together, it was clear his family favored Jaden, as they rarely engaged with Caleb or Callie. After seeing these interactions on multiple occasions, and since the kids were old enough to be alone, Tanesha let them stay home more often than not.

Tanesha always felt like she was fighting for fairness for "her" children.

Deep down, she knew that Jason saw "her" children as a burden, and he struggled to connect with them. She'd done everything right, waiting to introduce Jason to them when the relationship became serious, not moving him in before they got married, and even trying to create opportunities for everyone to connect through family vacations and outings.

Caleb and Callie's father wasn't physically present as much as Tanesha would've liked, but he did contribute financially. When she met Jason, she just knew he would be a great father figure for his kids, especially Caleb. When the two were dating, everything was fine, but once they got married and Jaden was born, the relationship between Jason and Caleb took a turn for the worse. Tanesha was tired of being in the middle and craved peace in her home.

Language Matters

In my work with blended families, I immediately notice the language used to describe the relationships. Often, I hear possessive language, like "my son," "my daughter," "my house," or detached language, like "her son," "his son," "his house," etc. We can quickly show our attachment or detachment to people and things. Not only do I hear this language in sessions, but these exact phrases are also said in the homes of blended families. What we say conveys how we feel and see situations.

When we say, "*Her* son never takes out the trash without being reminded at least five times," we're saying, "This isn't my son, and she needs to control him."

When we say, "This was my house before you moved in, and rules don't change overnight," we're saying, "I'm not willing to make adjustments to fit what you think is best."

Unity language sounds like "we," "the," "ours, they," or naming something directly.

Examples of Unity Language

"We need to talk about how to encourage him to be helpful without hounding him."

"The house rules need to be adjusted to encompass both of our parenting styles."

Parenting is a team sport, and parents, whether biological or step-, will differ. The best thing couples can do is practice understanding their partner and be flexible with how they parent. Many parenting books exist because it's such a complex and challenging relationship to manage. Although we know a great deal about what's harmful to children, no one knows the best way. When parenting with a partner, it's important to remember that your way isn't always best.

It's also essential to encourage extended family to use unity language. A family member might say something like "your wife's son." If so, correct them by saying "*our* son" or "my bonus son."

Connect Before You Direct

The biological parent benefits from the bonding time they've shared with their children. Therefore, when they correct their child, the child might receive it better than a correction from a stepparent. For successful relationships, stepparents must build connections with their stepchildren before doling out rules or implementing structure and discipline.

For any healthy relationships to develop, stepparents must build trust, consistency, understanding, and respect. Many times (far too many), I've found that stepparents believe they should be granted respect just because they're adults. Not true. The truth is that children are often compliant without being respectful. Since they can't control their environment, children consider basic compliance to be their next best option.

Since the adult is creating a new reality in the family, they should take charge of nurturing the relationship with the stepchild. There's no such thing as being there for the parent in a blended family without being there for the child.

For example, Sierra's daughter, Tam, was sixteen years old and had struggled with depression for years. Sierra's partner, Noelle, thought Tam was lazy and needed to be pushed to succeed. So Noelle pushed because Sierra wouldn't. The couple argued about the proper approach, and Noelle's lack of understanding about depression caused her to see Tam as lazy instead of as someone who was unmotivated simply due to her condition. Once the couple learned more about how teens are affected by depression, they sent Tam to therapy and implemented strategies to co-parent her.

Compassion is a central element for blending families successfully. Without compassion, it's easy to take offense. Building compassion helps forge nonjudgmental relationships.

Compliment Before You Critique

No one likes to hear how terribly they're performing a job. If you have a critique, issue a compliment first to soften the comment.

Examples of Compliment to Critique
- "Max is so intelligent. I'll bet if you allowed him to do more things independently, he'd be able to manage himself."

- "It's amazing how you've been able to manage Tam's depression. I think seeing a therapist together as a family could be another step in the right direction."
- "I love how close you are with your son, Steve. I have a feeling if we spoke to him lovingly and calmly about his behavior, he'd be willing to try to do better."
- "Tabbi loves when she has something to look forward to. I wonder if explaining what's next or what she might expect would help with her anxiety."

Treat Your Stepchildren Like You Would Treat Your Biological Children

Families exist before stepparents become a part of them, so it's impossible to expect significant changes to happen overnight. Stepparents are building a relationship that takes time. In stepfamilies, the attachment typically doesn't happen when a child is an infant because the introduction is later. It is possible to build a secure attachment when you are aware that you're entering at a later stage, knowledgeable of the child's love style, and patient with getting to know each other. The best way to proceed is with small steps in the right direction. What follows are some ways to take those small steps.

Don't Take Your Frustrations Out on Children

When a couple can't get into a healthy co-parenting rhythm, it's important that they not take their frustrations out on the children. After all, the kids didn't ask for the situation, and much of what the adults decide is out of their control. So in this situation, be accountable for your actions. Perfection isn't required, so if you happen to say the wrong thing or behave in a way you're not proud of, apologize. Children respect accountability, which shows them that you're not above reproach, and it teaches them to be accountable, too.

Avoid Blatant Differences in How Children Are Treated

Kyle stayed in his man cave most of the time, but when his two sons visited every other weekend, he spent time with them playing basketball, going to restaurants, and chatting. Lisa's two sons noticed that, in contrast, Kyle ignored them.

When we share a home with someone, engagement is essential. Ignoring certain household members is hurtful and doesn't help forge positive relationships. Even when children have the support of a parent outside the home, it's still vital for them to build a relationship with their stepparent. Neglect is unhealthy, and there's no such thing as too much love.

Don't Leave All the Parenting to Your Partner

Parenting is a duty, just like other duties in the home. When you decide to merge with another person who has children, it's likely there's an unspoken agreement that you'll connect your families. Therefore, the children become a collective responsibility, even if there's a shared custody arrangement with the biological parent. It isn't healthy to view children as "yours" and "theirs."

What to Do When You've Tried Everything, but the Kids Won't Let You In

Sometimes it's the children, not the adult, who give the stepparent a hard time despite their best efforts. It can be hard for children to accept a new person into their lives. Although they may not have the language to explain it, children might want to see if the stepparent is trustworthy and truly cares. For this reason, consistency is key. When an adult gives up too quickly, children believe that the adult's attempts to connect may have been disingenuous.

If attempts to connect with your stepchild fall flat even after trying, it may be necessary to seek family therapy to work through the child's issues around accepting you as the stepparent.

Dealing with Difficult Exes

Exes can make co-parenting challenging even without a blended family. Your partner may easily get fed up with your ex, who gets in the way of your household functioning.

When you have a difficult ex, try this:

- Affirm your partner's feelings, and don't stick up for your ex. Sometimes, a person's behavior is indeed problematic because they're hurt. However, it isn't OK for them to make your life more challenging. Affirming your partner's feelings can sound like, "I understand why you're frustrated," or "That was wrong, and it makes sense that you don't want to interact with them."
- Don't make passive-aggressive comments about the problematic parent around the children. Keep a united front, even when your ex or your partner's ex talks about you. It's imperative that you not vent in front of the children.
- Be clear with your ex about wanting the relationship to go smoothly for the children's sake. Be angry, but don't be petty. You might want revenge on your ex, but it will only make the situation worse.

- Your ex may be so challenging that a mediator or lawyer is the best option for communication and planning.
- Work on developing compassion toward your ex because you'll have a relationship with them indefinitely. When your children are adults, you'll likely be in the same spaces at celebrations and as grandparents. Start making peace, at least mentally, as soon as possible because you can't remove them from your life.

Loyalty

It isn't nice or fair, but some parents still force a child to pick sides. Without a parent saying so, children will pick a side because they don't understand the entirety of the situation. Adults should encourage children to have healthy relationships with all concerned, and not be mean or misbehave toward a stepparent.

For example, Joshua's father made it clear that his mother cheated and left the family. During his visits with his mother, he had behavioral issues because he was angry, believing she had broken up the family.

Adults do things that children can't understand, and it isn't in their best interest to know everything. It's best when parents focus on helping children process their feelings about the end of the parental relationship, as well as the different version of family life they must face, which doesn't include their parents living together.

Individual and family therapy are excellent tools to help a child transition immediately after a divorce and when they're conflicted about the need to be loyal. Additionally, parents and stepparents must be careful not to take the child's behavior personally. Instead, see the child's behavior as an unskilled way of dealing with a difficult situation.

Lack of Involvement (Financially or Physically)

When a stepparent does more for children (preparing meals, paying for living experiences, helping with homework, etc.) than the biological parent who lives outside the home, it can breed resentment from the ex or make the stepparent feel unappreciated.

For example, Bethany treated her stepdaughter, Haley, as one of her own, and she fell in love with her husband because of how much he loved his daughter. He was a great dad and had full custody. Haley's biological mother didn't show up for her daughter's games and rarely stuck to her commitment of taking Haley for full summers, some holidays, and every other weekend. Bethany often felt like she wasn't appreciated enough for everything she did for her stepdaughter. She felt conflicted and sad for Haley, and she was angry that her husband's ex refused to step up more often.

Children can't control what a parent does or doesn't do. So be careful not to become unintentionally passive-aggressive toward the child or your partner because you're frustrated with the ex's lack of involvement. If your stepchild doesn't show appreciation now, your efforts may be acknowledged in the future when they're more mature.

Family therapy can help ease the transition into blended family living. Be intentional about how you want to address the challenges within your blended family. Often, people ignore issues, which only makes them worse.

Talking about the elephant in the room might sound like this:

> To a stepchild: "I know that you love your mother, and you might feel like it's a betrayal to love me, too. I will love you no matter what, and it's OK for you to love more than one person."

To your partner: "My children can tell that you treat them
　　　differently from how you treat your children. Let's talk
　　　about how to treat both sets of children. Things won't be
　　　100 percent fair, but they can be less lopsided."

I've worked with many families who have blended successfully. In these
stories, parents were intentional about forging healthy relationships and
open to the discomfort of the many emotions felt by everyone involved.

EXERCISE

Grab your journal or a piece of paper to complete the following prompts:

* ❊ What challenges do you experience in your blended family?
* ❊ How do you manage the conflict in the co-parenting
  relationship?
* ❊ What do you need to accept about your family dynamic?

CHAPTER 17

The Beginning of a New Chapter

Family problems are taboo. Typically, people feel ashamed, so they keep secrets and ignore the issues in their family.

I've found comfort in relationships with friends who are transparent about the complexities of their relationships with siblings, parents, and beyond. Unfortunately, it's rare for people to be brave enough to risk the vulnerability of honesty.

As early as middle school, I sought out people who were brave enough to say, "My parents are on drugs," or "I haven't seen my father in years," or "My mother is dating a jerk." Children can be very candid when they find someone who will listen. I love sharing, and I love listening—because both are healing.

I've often seen people on social media attempt to fake it until they make it. Mother's Day seems to bring out an outpouring of inauthentic relationship depictions. I might see a long post with pictures describing someone's "perfect" relationship with their mother. I want these people to know that it's OK not to post inauthentic "heartfelt" messages just because they see others doing it. Seeing the so-called ideal experiences of others can be tough, but lying to ourselves and the world is much harder in the long run.

Inauthenticity becomes a big problem when we feel we must purchase a greeting card for a family member with whom we have a dysfunctional relationship. Picture it: you're trying to reconnect with your sister, but the cards don't quite capture the ups and downs of your relationship. I'm not advocating for a card line for dysfunctional families, but the lack of acknowledgment of complex relationships can be triggering when you're sifting through cards at the store or online. No one talks about how hard it is to find a card for a parent with whom you don't have a healthy relationship. Greeting cards are geared toward healthy relationships, and it can be sad to be reminded of what you don't have. It's OK if you don't find the perfect card to fit your situation.

When I started talking openly on social media about dysfunctional families, I was surprised by the number of people who connected with the content. Many of my posts start with "When you're from a dysfunctional family . . ." These are personal narratives about how to coexist, accept, and gather ourselves. Brave people liked, saved, and shared the posts. People sent me messages about how my words helped them change in ways they didn't know they needed. Once, a person sent me a message about how she shared my posts with her mother, and it sparked a conversation that changed their relationship for the better. It isn't all roses, of course. I've had to delete comments from people who shamed others for leaving unhealthy relationships or acknowledging they had dysfunctional relationships.

Sometimes, it can be challenging for people who haven't experienced a dysfunctional family to understand someone else's choices. When people have no frame of reference, we give our power away if we try to convince them to understand us. Let them have their story while you keep yours. It isn't always possible or necessary to convert people, and it can be peaceful to let go of trying to reach an agreement. The way you choose to deal with your family may look different from how others choose to deal with theirs. Neither needs to be seen as right or wrong, and can simply be accepted as different.

Shame keeps us silent. We need more people to speak up about their families and as a tool for fostering intentional connections. Someone once told me, "No one else knows my mother is an alcoholic, and I'm too ashamed to tell anyone." This person often felt disconnected in their relationships because people didn't know about an important part of their life. They told others a fictional version.

When there is one, there are many. We find others like us through intentional honesty.

When you're from a dysfunctional family, choosing to stay away from drama might require missing family events. Presumably, you've learned that the same ending occurs event after event, and you don't want to be involved. It's typical for some people in your family to struggle to understand your desire for peace over chaos. They've become accustomed to the chaos and don't realize they have the power to say no to drama.

It's a conscious choice to be a part of drama and chaos. We have to learn to choose what's best for us when situations don't change for the better. It takes practice to get comfortable with making such hard choices.

It's a conscious choice to be a part of drama and chaos.

The following IG post is what I wanted to say to a family member who had made excuses for themself and downplayed my hard work to break the cycle within our family. I didn't end up saying it to them because it had already been said to them before.

REPEAT AFTER ME

"I am no longer a child in a dysfunctional home. I'm an adult with the ability to make healthy choices, create boundaries, and live the life that I create. Just because we haven't been taught something, it isn't a reason to continue not knowing. I

will no longer use the excuse 'My parents never taught me
_____' as a reason to not do better. I can teach myself by read-
ing, being open to learning, being curious, and connecting to
healthy people. I can find support through mentors, role models, elders, or mental health professionals. I can learn things
that I was never taught, including how to be in healthy
relationships, how to feel, how to care for myself, how to be assertive, and how to deal with problems in a healthy way."

It isn't easy to make changes, but it's possible. At least ten years
ago, while journaling, I wrote a list of generational patterns I wanted to
break. People stay the same when we don't actively choose to do anything
different. Hoping that they will become different isn't something we can
manifest. Change comes from practicing new habits and traditions while
building a healthy support system.

No two situations are the same, and the solutions are not one-size-fits-
all. In some cases, you may choose to end a relationship, while in others,
you might decide to continue while maintaining healthy boundaries. You
are on your own timeline—not mine, not your partner's, not your therapist's, or anyone else's. You have to be comfortable with the decision you
make, and some decisions are harder than others.

You can revisit this book whenever you need it, and trust me, you'll
need it again and again as a reminder to create relationships that nurture
your mental health. Be the change you wish to see in your family. Changing yourself is the only thing that's possible.

Be the change you wish to see in your family.

Reframing, shifting your expectations,
placing boundaries, curating community,
and taking care of yourself will ultimately be your freedom from what you
can't control.

Frequently Asked Questions

Is it enabling if I continue a relationship with my mom even though she hasn't changed?

The relationship between parent and child is a unique bond, and even when parents don't change, many people will continue the relationship. This isn't enabling; it's hoping for change.

Enabling is about your behavior in the relationship. Do you support them in harming themselves or someone else? Do you ignore or minimize behaviors that should be addressed? If not, you're simply maintaining a relationship with someone whose behavior you wish were different.

Consider This: Ending a relationship isn't a requirement; it's an option you may not choose to exercise with your mother, and that's OK.

My parent is eighty years old and an alcoholic. I'm angry. Can I tell them?

Yes, you can share how their alcoholism makes you feel and how it has impacted your life. It can be a relief to release this anger if you've held it inside. However, if you're hoping that sharing your issues will change them, be clear about that in your conversation, while also understanding that eliminating alcohol is your parent's choice. They might not see it as an easy process.

Al-Anon is a group with chapters throughout the world that can help you receive support from others who are adult children of alcoholics. Part of this process is learning how to better parent yourself. Find support via this group, or work individually with a therapist.

Consider This: Take care of yourself by managing your mental health. Adult Children of Alcoholics: https://adultchildren.org

Al-Anon: https://al-anon.org

My father was abusive (verbally, mentally, and physically) when I was a child. He justifies his actions because he believes they were appropriate. He wants a relationship with my children. How do I protect them from what I experienced? He currently has limited access.

When people haven't changed, it's hard to determine how to be in a relationship with them, and safety is a significant concern when they try to justify their abusive actions. You didn't feel safe, and you're unsure if your kids will be safe. As the parent, it's your job to protect them whenever you can.

Consider This: Based on the knowledge you have about your father, you're keeping him away from them, which seems like the safest option for now.

I want my mother to get help for her mental health. How can I make her talk to a therapist?

It can be hard watching a loved one suffer while knowing that they can get better with therapy. But we can't convince people to go to a therapist if they don't want to go. Besides, your mother may not receive what she needs from the process if she has been forced into it.

Let's be honest: the vulnerability required in therapy is hard even when people seek it out themselves. You can't make a person ready simply because you're prepared for them to change.

Consider This: Based on her current behavior, what type of relationship can you have with her despite her mental health issues?

My mother-in-law and sister-in-law are phony. Do I have to maintain a relationship with them?

You can be cordial to your in-laws without having a close relationship. Control what you do on your end. For example, you don't have to reach out to chat about nonessential topics, and you don't have to invite them to personal events such as your birthday party.

Consider This: Do you want to maintain inauthentic relationships?

How do I handle my spouse cutting ties with their siblings and family?

Support your partner by asking them what they need and listening when they want to share how they feel about the estrangement. People have a long history with their families, and you may not understand everything from your point of view.

Even when family members have changed, your partner might not want to maintain relationships with them. You can still support your partner, even if they make a different choice than you feel you would make. Sometimes, we have to respect someone's decision without understanding all the reasons behind it.

Consider This: How does the shift in family dynamics impact your relationship with your partner?

My stepdaughter is a liar. My partner doesn't discipline her daughter for lying, and it causes us to argue constantly. How can we get on the same page about discipline?

Both of you have work to do. You need to develop an empathetic relationship with your stepdaughter, while your partner should address the lack of honesty. It's important to know why your child might be choosing to be dishonest (i.e., what they are getting from that behavior), and it is essential to show her you'll love her no matter what. People are dishonest, not just children. Some may normalize lying as a way to protect themselves from consequences. In many households, parents disagree about what's appropriate in terms of discipline. Lead with love and compassion, and leave the discipline to your partner until you have a healthier relationship with your stepdaughter.

Consider This: Your stepdaughter is trying to communicate something through her behavior. What is she saying?

How do I handle my dad's disapproval of my lifestyle?

It would be nice if your parent approved of all your choices, but likely, they won't. Your dad would probably say that he wants you to be happy. Perhaps a part of your happiness is choosing to do something that he doesn't approve of. It might be helpful to have a conversation about how to respect your choices even if he disapproves of them.

Consider This: You're an adult and entitled to make your own choices.

My mom texts me too much, and our relationship is strained. How should I address this with her?

Is your mother aware of your feelings about the relationship? Have you asked her to stop texting so much? Are you responding to the texts? This might give a false impression that you're more involved than you'd like to be. You may be demonstrating that you don't want a closer relationship with her, and it seems like she is ignoring that. A small step in the right direction could be making a gentle request that she does not text you as much because it's causing you some anxiety. Perhaps that statement will lead to a meaningful conversation, and either way, it will make her aware of your expectation.

Consider This: She's creating the type of relationship she wants with you, but you want something different.

Acknowledgments

Thousands of people have liked my social media posts and sent DMs and emails about how my words about dysfunctional families have made them feel seen and less alone in a world that clamors toward ideal family stereotypes. Nearly every place you look—on TV, in magazines, and on social media—there's an overflow of picture-perfect families. When you have a dysfunctional family, it's easy to believe that you are alone. But you are not. In the comfort of healthy relationships with friends and some family members, I began sharing my honest thoughts about dysfunctional relationships with relatives. To all the people who've come across my work, I thank you for being brave enough to keep reading, and I hope you feel moved enough to apply what feels right for you from this book.

To my husband, our lives have changed so much since my work has become popular, and you've made intentional adjustments to create room for me and my ambitions. Thank you for pushing me to be braver in my endeavors and for rising with me. To my daughters, I hope the cycles I broke in my family have a profound impact on what you're able to achieve in your life. My greatest inspiration for breaking cycles has been becoming a mother and wanting something better for not just myself but all of us. To my parents, thank you for being my street team—when they see you, they hear about me. There are people I will never meet who know my name and are proud of me because of your enthusiasm to share my work with others.

To my chosen family (friends), our time together has saved me in ways that I did not know I needed until I had it. My close friendships feel like sisterhoods, and I know that because we've cultivated something deep and authentic. I believe in creating what you need, and Darnell, a surrogate uncle and longtime neighbor, has always treated me like a niece, from patiently helping me learn to drive to rooting me on through every phase of adulthood.

Laura Lee Mattingly (my agent), we've been busy since *Set Boundaries, Find Peace*, and we keep coming up with ideas. You have helped me think through and develop some of my best work. I genuinely appreciate your industry expertise. Marian Lizzi, you are the easiest editor to work with, and even your corrections are kind and thoughtful. You have trusted my voice as an expert and shown me the importance of speaking directly from my professional experiences. Thank you to Marian's team, Jess Morphew (art director), and Natasha Soto (editorial assistant) for guiding me through this process. My entire Penguin Random House team, Roshe Anderson, Marlena Brown, Sara Johnson, Lindsay Gordon, and Carla Iannone, has been instrumental in marketing and sustaining my writing projects. Britney Irving, you read the first draft of this book and gave me such excellent feedback. Thank you for keeping my schedule nice and boundaried and providing valuable insight. Thank you, Shaunsie Reed, for helping build my work from the beginning. You arrived when we had very little work to do; now we're overflowing.

Writing this book has been an accountability tool. Therapy has been a fantastic outlet over the years and continues to be a huge source of self-care for me. My therapist asked me, "Why do you have a relationship with this person?" I, too, had to own when I wasn't ready to leave or change my role in unhealthy family relationships. Thank you to my therapist, who patiently waited with me as I struggled to make hard and necessary changes.

Further Reading

Introduction

Holt-Lundstad, Julianne, Timothy B. Smith, and J. Bradley Layton. "Social Relationships and Mortality Risk: A Meta-analytic Review." *PLoS Medicine*, July 27, 2010. https://journals.plos.org/plosmedicine/article?id=10.1371/journal.pmed.1000316.

Weir, Kristen. "Life-saving Relationships." *Monitor on Psychology* 49, no. 3 (March 2018). https://www.apa.org/monitor/2018/03/life-saving-relationships.

Chapter 1: What Dysfunction Looks Like

Clements, Ron, and John Musker, dirs. *The Little Mermaid*, two-disc platinum ed. Burbank, CA: Walt Disney Home Entertainment, 2006.

Collins, Stephanie D. Baker. "From Homeless Teen to Chronically Homeless Adult: A Qualitative Study of the Impact of Childhood Events on Adult Homelessness." https://ojs.uwindsor.ca/index.php/csw/article/download/5882/4872?inline=1.

Ewing, Heidi, and Rachel Grady, dirs. *The Boys of Baraka*. New York: Think Film, Loki Films, and Independent Television Service, 2005.

Harrison, Thomas F., and Hilary S. Connery. *The Complete Family Guide to Addiction: Everything You Need to Know Now to Help Your Loved One and Yourself.* New York: Guilford Press, 2019.

John, Oliver P., and James J. Gross. "Healthy and Unhealthy Emotion Regulation: Personality Processes, Individual Differences, and Life Span Development." *Journal of Personality* 72, no. 6 (December 2004): 1301–34. https://doi.org/10.1111/j.1467-6494.2004.00298.x, PMID: 15509284.

Married . . . with Children. Culver City, CA: Columbia TriStar Home Entertainment, 1987–1997.

McLaughlin, Katie. "The Long Shadow of Adverse Childhood Experiences." *Psychological Science Agenda*, April 2017. https://www.apa.org/science/about/psa /2017/04/adverse-childhood.

Perry, Bruce D., and Oprah Winfrey. *What Happened to You?: Conversations on Trauma, Resilience, and Healing.* New York: Flatiron Books, 2021.

Radcliff, Elizabeth, Elizabeth Crouch, Melissa Strompolis, and Aditi Srivastav. "Homelessness in Childhood and Adverse Childhood Experiences (ACEs)." *Maternal and Child Health Journal* 23 (2019): 811–20. https://doi.org/10.1007 /s10995-018-02698-w.

van der Kolk, Bessel. *The Body Keeps the Score: Brain, Mind, and Body in the Healing of Trauma.* New York: Viking Press, 2014.

Winfrey, Oprah. *The Oprah Winfrey Show.* Hollywood, CA: Harpo Productions and Paramount Pictures, 1986–2011.

Yale Medicine. "Parental Depression: How It Affects a Child." https://www .yalemedicine.org/conditions/how-parental-depression-affects-child.

Chapter 2: Boundary Violations, Codependency, and Enmeshment

Campbell, Sherrie. *But It's Your Family: Cutting Ties with Toxic Family Members and Loving Yourself in the Aftermath.* New York: Morgan James Publishing, 2019.

Chapter 3: Addiction, Neglect, and Abuse

Black, Claudia. *"It Will Never Happen to Me!": Children of Alcoholics—as Youngsters, Adolescents, Adults.* New York: Ballantine Books, 1987.

Boston University Medical Center. "Child/Teen Sexual and Physical Abuse Linked to Fibroids in Premenopausal Women." ScienceDaily, December 17, 2010. https://www.sciencedaily.com/releases/2010/11/101115111011.htm.

Boynton-Jarrett, Renée, Janet W. Rich-Edwards, Hee-Jin Jun, Eileen N. Hibert, and Rosalind J. Wright. "Abuse in Childhood and Risk of Uterine Leiomyoma: The Role of Emotional Support in Biologic Resilience." *Epidemiology* 22, no. 1 (January 2011). https://doi.org/10.1097/EDE.0b013e3181ffb172.

Canadian Association for Neuroscience. "Addiction as a Disorder of Decision-Making." ScienceDaily, May 22, 2013. Retrieved June 15, 2022. https://www .sciencedaily.com/releases/2013/05/130522095809.htm.

Christakis, Erika. "The Dangers of Distracted Parenting." *The Atlantic,* July–August 2018. https://www.theatlantic.com/magazine/archive/2018/07/the -dangers-of-distracted-parenting/561752.

Dinneen, Allyson. *Notes from Your Therapist.* Irvine, CA: Harvest, 2020.

Eger, Edith Eva, with Esmé Schwall Weigand and a foreword by Philip Zimbardo. *The Choice: Embrace the Possible.* New York: Scribner, 2017.

Green, Kelly E. *Relationships in Recovery: Repairing Damage and Building Healthy Connections While Overcoming Addiction.* New York: Guilford Press, 2021.

Imperial College London. "Gambling Addiction Triggers the Same Brain Areas as Drug and Alcohol Cravings: Gambling Addiction Activates the Same Brain Pathways as Drug and Alcohol Cravings, Suggests New Research." Science-Daily. January 3, 2017. Retrieved June 15, 2022. https://www.sciencedaily.com/releases/2017/01/170103101751.htm.

Luthar, Suniya S., and Shawn J. Latendresse. "Children of the Affluent: Challenges to Well-Being." *Current Directions in Psychological Science* 14, no. 1 (February 2005): 49–53. https://doi.org/10.1111/j.0963-7214.2005.00333.x.

University at Buffalo Research Institute on Addictions. "RIA Reaching Others: Does Drinking Affect Marriage?" Fall 2014. https://www.buffalo.edu/content/dam/www/ria/PDFs/ES12-MarriageandDrinking.pdf.

University of Manchester. "Child Abuse Linked to Risk of Suicide in Later Life." ScienceDaily, January 9, 2019. https://www.sciencedaily.com/releases/2019/01/190109192533.htm.

University of North Carolina at Chapel Hill. "Severe PMS Linked with Physical, Sexual Abuse in Childhood." ScienceDaily, November 13, 1998. Retrieved June 14, 2022. https://www.sciencedaily.com/releases/1998/11/981113082005.htm.

Wiley-Blackwell. "Abuse in Childhood Linked to Migraine and Other Pain Disorders." ScienceDaily, January 6, 2010. Retrieved June 15, 2022. https://www.sciencedaily.com/releases/2010/01/100106003608.htm.

Chapter 4: Repeating the Cycle

George Mason University. "Grandfamilies: New Study Uncovers Common Themes and Challenges in Kinship Care." ScienceDaily, May 5, 2020. Retrieved June 15, 2022. https://www.sciencedaily.com/releases/2020/05/200505164629.htm.

Georgia State University. "Solo Grandparents Raising Grandchildren at Greater Risk Than Parents for Serious Health Problems." ScienceDaily, September 14, 2015. https://www.sciencedaily.com/releases/2015/09/150914152912.htm.

Hendrix, Harville. *Getting the Love You Want: A Guide for Couples.* New York: Perennial Library, 2007.

University of Missouri–Columbia. "Emotional Disconnection Disorder Threatens Marriages, Researcher Says." ScienceDaily, November 12, 2012. https://www.sciencedaily.com/releases/2012/11/121112171321.htm.

University of Oxford. "Grandma and Grandpa Are Good for Children." ScienceDaily, June 7, 2008. Retrieved June 15, 2022. https://www.sciencedaily.com/releases/2008/06/080605091358.htm.

Chapter 5: Trauma Across Generations

American Addiction Centers. "Depression & Substance Abuse," 2022. https://americanaddictioncenters.org/treating-depression-substance-abuse.

———. "Post-Traumatic Stress Disorder (PTSD) & Addiction: Signs, Symptoms & Treatment," 2022. https://americanaddictioncenters.org/co-occurring-disorders/ptsd-addiction.

American Psychiatric Association. *Diagnostic and Statistical Manual of Mental Disorders,* 5th ed. Washington, DC: The American Psychiatric Association, 2013.

DeGruy, Joy. *Post Traumatic Slave Syndrome: America's Legacy of Enduring Injury and Healing.* Milwaukie, OR: Uptone Press, 2005; direct quote at https://en.wikipedia.org/wiki/Post_Traumatic_Slave_Syndrome.

National Center on Substance Abuse and Child Warfare. "Child Welfare and Alcohol and Drug Use Statistics." https://ncsacw.acf.hhs.gov/research/child-welfare-and-treatment-statistics.aspx.

Yapko, Michael D. *Depression Is Contagious: How the Most Common Mood Disorder Is Spreading Around the World and How to Stop It.* New York: Atria Books, 2013.

Chapter 8: How to Manage Relationships with People Who Won't Change

Kubrick, Stanley, dir. *Full Metal Jacket.* Burbank, CA: Warner Bros., 1987.

University College London. "'Fat Shaming' Doesn't Encourage Weight Loss." ScienceDaily, September 10, 2014. Retrieved June 16, 2022. https://www.sciencedaily.com/releases/2014/09/140910214151.htm.

University of Michigan. "Shame on Us: Shaming Some Kids Makes Them More Aggressive." December 19, 2008. https://news.umich.edu/shame-on-us-shaming-some-kids-makes-them-more-aggressive.

Vitug, Jason. *You Only Live Once: The Roadmap to Financial Wellness and a Purposeful Life.* Hoboken, NJ: Wiley, 2016.

Chapter 9: Ending Relationships When Others Won't Change

Lowe, Lindsay. "Oprah Winfrey Opens Up About the Emotional Days Before Her Mother's Death." *Today,* December 12, 2018. https://www.today.com/parents/oprah-opens-about-her-mother-s-death-people-interview-t145038.

Pillemer, Karl. *Fault Lines: Fractured Families and How to Mend Them.* New York: Avery, 2020.

University of Michigan. "Step Back to Move Forward Emotionally, Study Suggests." ScienceDaily, September 24, 2008. Retrieved June 15, 2022. https://www.sciencedaily.com/releases/2008/09/080923122006.htm.

Walls, Jeanette. *The Glass Castle: A Memoir.* New York: Scribner, 2006.

Chapter 11: Troubleshooting Relationships with Parents

Brooks, Arthur C. "The Key to a Good Parent-Child Relationship? Low Expectations." *The Atlantic,* May 12, 2022. https://www.theatlantic.com/family/archive/2022/05/parents-adult-children-lower-your-expectations/629830/.

Cori, Jasmin Lee. *The Emotionally Absent Mother: How to Recognize and Heal the Invisible Effects of Childhood Emotional Neglect.* New York: Experiment, 2017.

Gibson, Lindsay C. *Adult Children of Emotionally Immature Parents: How to Heal from Distant, Rejecting, or Self-Involved Parents.* Brattleboro, VT: Echo Point Books and Media, 2021.

McBride, Karyl. *Will I Ever Be Good Enough?: Healing the Daughters of Narcissistic Mothers.* New York: Free Press, 2009.

Society for Personality and Social Psychology. "Sometimes Expressing Anger Can Help a Relationship in the Long-Term." ScienceDaily, August 2, 2012. Retrieved July 14, 2022. https://www.sciencedaily.com/releases/2012/08/120802133649.htm.

Webb, Jonice, with Christine Musello. *Running on Empty: Overcome Your Childhood Emotional Neglect.* New York: Morgan James, 2013.

Chapter 12: Troubleshooting Relationships with Siblings

Faber, Adele, and Elaine Mazlish. *Siblings Without Rivalry: How to Help Your Children Live Together So You Can Live Too.* New York: Simon & Schuster, 1987.

Perry, Phillipa. *The Book You Wish Your Parents Had Read (and Your Children Will Be Glad That You Did).* New York: Penguin Life, 2020.

University of California, Berkeley. "Gossip Can Have Social and Psychological Benefits." ScienceDaily, January 18, 2012. Retrieved July 13, 2022. https://www.sciencedaily.com/releases/2012/01/120117145103.htm.

Chapter 13: Troubleshooting Relationships with Children

Coleman, Joshua. *Rules of Estrangement: Why Adult Children Cut Ties and How to Heal the Conflict.* London: Sheldon Press, 2021.

————. *When Parents Hurt: Compassionate Strategies When You and Your Grown Child Don't Get Along.* New York: HarperCollins, 2014.

Mason, Paul T., and Randi Kreger. *Stop Walking on Eggshells: Taking Your Life Back When Someone You Care About Has Borderline Personality Disorder.* Oakland, CA: New Harbinger, 2010.

Chapter 16: Managing Blended Families

Murray, Stephanie H. "The Stepparent's Dilemma." *The Atlantic*, April 19, 2022. https://www.theatlantic.com/family/archive/2022/04/stepparenting -kids-advice-nacho-disengage/629600.

Index

About Nedra

Nedra Glover Tawwab, MSW, LCSW, is a *New York Times* bestselling author, licensed therapist, and sought-after relationship expert. She has practiced relationship therapy for fifteen years and is the founder and owner of the group therapy practice Kaleidoscope Counseling. Every day she helps people create healthy relationships by teaching them how to implement boundaries. Her philosophy is that a lack of boundaries and assertiveness underlie most relationship issues, and her gift is helping people create healthy relationships with themselves and others.

Nedra earned her undergraduate and graduate degrees from Wayne State University, in Detroit, Michigan. She has additional certifications in working with families and couples and in perinatal mood and anxiety disorders, plus advanced training for counseling adults who've experienced childhood emotional neglect.

Nedra has appeared as an expert on *Red Table Talk*, *The Breakfast Club*, *Good Morning America*, and *CBS Mornings*, to name a few. Her work has been highlighted in *The New York Times*, *The Guardian*, and *Vice* and has appeared on numerous podcasts, including *Good Life Project*, *Sofia with an F*, and *Life Kit*. She runs a popular Instagram account where she shares practices, tools, and reflections for mental health and hosts weekly Q&As.

Also by **NEDRA GLOVER TAWWAB**